MW01131112

365 Jataka Tales

and other stories

OM
KIDZ

An imprint of Om Books International

Reprinted 2009

Published by

Om KIDZ is an Imprint of Om Books International

Corporate & Editorial Office
A-12, Sector 64, Noida - 201 301
Uttar Pradesh, India
Phone: +91-120-477 4100

Sales Office
4379/4B, Prakash House, Ansari Road
Darya Ganj, New Delhi - 110 002, India
Phone: +91-11-2326 3363, 2326 5303
Fax: +91-11-2327 8091

Email: sales@ombooks.com
Website: www.ombooks.com

ISBN 978-81-87107-57-6

Printed by Tien Wah (PTE) Ltd

10 9 8 7 6 5 4 3 2

365

Jataka Tales

and other stories

Contents

The Story of the Month: Prince Wicked and the Grateful Animals

The Story of the Month

Prince Wicked and the Grateful Animals

01 Prince Wicked and the Grateful Animals

Long ago there lived a very selfish prince called Prince Wicked. Everybody hated him for his haughty and cruel nature. One day while Prince Wicked was swimming in the river, a violent storm swept him away. "Let's leave him here and go back to the palace," said the servants and, without making any effort to save the drowning prince, returned to the palace. "Save me," cried the prince and held on to a floating log. Meanwhile a rat and a snake, whose homes were filled with water, also sought shelter in the log. As they were floating together, a parrot whose tree was uprooted in the storm, flew in to join them. Now all the four floated on the turbulent waters of the river. "Help… else we'll drown," shouted the prince as the water level rose. A poor fisherman, who was standing outside his hut, heard the prince and ran to help him. He jumped into the river and pulled Prince Wicked and the three animals ashore. He took them home and made them warm by the fire. The fisherman appeared more concerned about the animals and this annoyed the arrogant prince. He said to himself, "How dare he give more importance to these animals instead of me. Doesn't he know I'm a prince?"

Back in the palace, the king looked everywhere for the prince but failed to find him. Meanwhile the storm subsided and the snake, the rat, the parrot and the prince decided to return to their homes. Before leaving, the snake told the fisherman to call him if he wanted to know about hidden treasures, the rat asked the fisherman to call him if he needed gold coins which were hidden in the rat's hole and the parrot asked the fisherman to call him if he needed grains of his choice. Seeing this, Prince Wicked also reluctantly promised to reward the fisherman with riches as a mark of his gratitude. Days passed and Prince Wicked became the king. He forgot all about the fisherman saving his life and his promise. One day as the king was taking an elephant ride, he saw the fisherman who had saved his life, coming towards him. He remembered his promise and thinking that the fisherman had come to ask for the riches, he ordered his soldiers to arrest the fisherman and beat him to death. "Better to save animals rather than an ungrateful prince," the fisherman cried aloud as the king's soldiers beat him up. Hearing him, a few wise men who were watching the incident asked the fisherman what he meant. The fisherman then narrated how he had saved the prince along with a snake, a rat and a parrot and all about the prince's promise. Hearing him, the wise men decided to banish the wicked prince for his cruelty and make the fisherman their king. The poor fisherman was a noble soul and ruled the kingdom well. He went to the snake, the rat and the parrot and having collected whatever they had offered him as promised, he returned to the palace with his three grateful friends. He built a golden tube for the snake, a glass box for the rat and a golden tree for the parrot in his palace and they all lived happily ever after.

02 The Superstitious Brahmin

The Bodhisattva was once born as a Brahmin and lived in the Himavanta forest. One day, he went to the king's palace and was invited to stay in the royal park. There he saw a Brahmin sleeping under a tree. Suddenly the Brahmin awoke and took off his shawl. "Oh no! My shawl has been gnawed by rats. I'm sure this is the indication of some evil omen. Need to get rid of this rat-bitten shawl," shouted the Brahmin and called his son. "Throw this shawl away in the river to avoid any disaster," said the Brahmin throwing the shawl at his son. The shawl went flying and fell near the Bodhisattva, who picked it up and said, "Learned man, this shawl holds no evil omen. The rats might have been looking for food and just gnawed your shawl. No wise man should believe in omens." But the superstitious Brahmin was not convinced and handed the shawl to his son who went and threw it in the river.

03 The Story of a Tigress

The Bodhisattva was once born a scholar and mastered all the scriptures. He became an ascetic and had a number of disciples. One day, while the Bodhisattva was walking through the forest with his disciple Ajita, he saw a hungry tigress about to eat her own cubs. Deeply moved, Bodhisattva decided to offer himself as food for the tigress. Fearing that his disciple would stop him from sacrificing his life, the Bodhisattva sent Ajita away on some pretext and placed himself in front of the tigress. "Grrr…" growled the tigress and ripped the Bodhisattva apart. She and her cubs fed on him ravenously. When Ajita returned and saw his master's blood-stained clothes, he shouted out in terror, "Good Gracious! These are Master's clothes. That means these creatures must have fed on him…"

With a heavy heart Ajita returned to narrate how his master had sacrificed his life out of charity and compassion.

04 A Precious Life

The Bodhisattva was once born as a deer. Every animal in the forest admired his handsome looks. One day, a prince came to hunt in the forest. "This forest is a good hunting ground," remarked the prince when he saw the surrounding greenery with many birds chirping overhead and a variety of animals running around. The prince's eyes fell on the deer and he followed it, aiming his bow and arrow. The charioteer drove the chariot at a breakneck speed but the deer ran even faster. Suddenly one of the wheels of the chariot came off and "Plop!" the prince fell headlong into the nearby river. "Help… Someone get me out, else I'll drown," shouted the frightened prince who did not know how to swim. The deer, who was nearby, heard the prince's cries and dragged him out of the water. Seeing that he was saved by the very deer he had wanted to shoot, the prince felt ashamed and vowed never to hunt animals.

05 The Wind and the Moon

Once there lived two very close friends—a lion and a tiger. They had been friends since they were cubs and didn't know that they were different from each other. They lived happily in a mountain forest which was also inhabited by a wise and gentle hermit. One day, the tiger and the lion entered into an argument as to whether the cold season starts when the new moon becomes a full moon or when the full moon becomes a new moon. The petty argument turned into a quarrel with each trying to prove the other wrong. So the two friends went to the wise hermit to ask him who was right. The hermit listened to both of them and said, "The cold season begins when cold winds blow and this can happen during any phase of the moon. So, in a way, both of you are right and in future, you should never quarrel, as unity brings happiness," said the hermit. "Oh… We were so silly," thought the two friends and decided never to argue over trivial matters.

06 The Straw Worth More than Gold

A shifty ascetic lived as a guest in the house of a rich man. One day the king needed to hide a box of gold coins. Thinking that he was a holy man who had renounced worldly pleasures, the rich man buried the gold coins in the ascetic's room. The ascetic smiled and pretending to be indifferent to the wealth said, "All these worldly things are of little interest to me." But when the rich man left, the crafty ascetic dug up the gold coins and hid them under a tree outside his hut. Next day, on the pretext of taking a pilgrimage, the ascetic took the rich man's leave and left his house with the gold coins. After a while, the ascetic returned with a straw and handed it to the rich man saying that he would not carry anything with him that belonged to others. The Bodhisattva, who was reborn as a merchant, saw this and sensing some foul play, asked the rich man to check if his gold coins were safe. Finding the gold coins missing, he declared the ascetic a cheat and got him imprisoned.

07 The Crab and the Crane

It was a hot summer without rains and the ponds had all dried up. Life became difficult for the fish in the ponds. A crane volunteered to take them to a pond in the deep woods where there was plenty of water. Distrustful of the crane the fish held a conference. At last a big fish went with the crane. "Look at that! It's so full of water," exclaimed the big fish with delight. "Yes, indeed. If you want I can carry you all, one by one, to this pond," suggested the crane. Desperate for a home, the fish decided to trust the crane. But alas, the crane took them to the woods and one by one ate them all up. Nothing but their bones remained. The last creature left in the pond was a crab. The crane took the crab, too, with him. But, as he was about to devour him, the crab clawed him so hard that his head broke off and the wicked crane died.

08 Sama, the Good Son

A divine couple had a son who was born with a golden skin. They called him Sama. Time passed and Sama grew up to be an obedient son. One day, Sama's parents got drenched in the rain and sought shelter under a tree. The water dripping from their bodies fell on a snake sleeping near an anthill. Angry at being disturbed, the snake spit out its poisonous venom which made the couple blind. From that day onwards, Sama looked after his blind parents.

One hot summer afternoon, Sama went to fetch some water from the lake in the nearby forest. The king, too, went hunting in that forest and mistaking Sama to be a goblin, shot his arrow at Sama. "Ouch…" Sama cried out in pain and fell dead. A fairy was watching the entire incident and persuaded the king to go to Sama's parents and confess what he had done. Meanwhile, the fairy with her magic wand brought Sama back to life and when his parents came to the lake, she cured their blindness too.

09 The Whatnot Tree

A merchant along with his caravan was once travelling through the forest. When darkness fell, he had to stop for the night under a tree loaded with fruits. The merchant examined the ripe fruits and realising it to be that of the poisonous Whatnot tree he warned his men not to pluck any fruits. But some of his servants greedily plucked the ripe fruits and ate them. The poisoned fruits caused their death. But the few who did not eat the fruit were safe.

Next morning, the villagers residing nearby, saw the merchant's men and wondered how they had escaped being poisoned by the fruits of the Whatnot tree. "I could make out the danger from the fact that ripe fruits were hanging from the tree without being touched, which is unusual," said the merchant and everybody appreciated his wisdom.

10 The Stupid Son

Once there lived a carpenter who had a shiny bald head. Whenever the carpenter came out in the sun, his bald head would shine like a mirror. Often, people would shade their eyes while talking to him on sunny days. One day, the carpenter was making a wooden bed. While he was sawing the wood, a mosquito, catching sight of his shiny head thought, "Let me sit on this bald head and enjoy a sumptuous meal," and flew towards it. When the mosquito started biting, the carpenter felt irritated and tried to chase it away with his hand. Though the mosquito flew away, it was reluctant to leave and kept coming back. The carpenter then called his son and asked him to help him get rid of the mosquito. "Don't worry Father, I'll kill him with one blow," said the son and hit hard with his hand. The mosquito was killed, but alas, the carpenter's head received a mighty knock!

11 A Huge Lump of Gold

A rich man once buried a huge lump of gold in his field to protect it from robbers. Years passed and the rich man forgot about it. Many years later a poor farmer was ploughing the plot of land and found the treasure. "Good Lord! Who has buried such a huge lump of gold in the field," the farmer wondered. Thinking it unsafe to carry it in broad daylight, the farmer buried it again and returned in the night to take it home. He tried to lift it, but it was too heavy for him. He tried dragging it with ropes, but that too was unsuccessful. Exhausted, the farmer sat down and tried to figure out a way to carry the lump of gold home. "I'll divide the lump into four halves and use each part for a different purpose," thought the farmer and broke it into four slabs of equal size. He carried them home one by one and from then on the poor farmer became a rich man.

12 The Power of Generosity

Once there lived a rich man who was famous for his charitable acts. He always gave alms to the poor. A poor hermit happened to be his neighbour. The hermit was called the Silent Buddha, for he was an enlightened person and spent all his time in meditation. Once he meditated for seven days and seven nights at a stretch without food or water. When he awoke from his trance, he was so hungry that he felt faint. The Silent Buddha went to the rich man to beg for food. Mara, the god of death, was jealous of the rich man's reputation and decided to stop him from giving alms and let the Silent Buddha die of starvation. When the rich man came forward to offer alms to the Silent Buddha, Mara lit a huge fire in between the two. But the rich man was determined and trusting the strength of his good deeds, walked through the fire and, emerging unharmed, offered the Silent Buddha food. Mara was defeated and departed saying, "Indeed the power of generosity is great."

13 The Quails and the Hunter

Once there was a clever quail hunter who was skilled at mimicking quail calls. He was able to catch many birds in this way. King Quail was worried about the falling number of quails. One day, he called for a meeting with all the quails in his nation and said, "My dear fellow quails! This is the time to show solidarity. Tomorrow when the hunter comes to catch us, we all will raise our heads in unison and fly away with the net to save our lives." The plan succeeded and in the following days the hunter couldn't catch even a single quail. But after a few days the hunter returned and tried to lure a group of quails. A quail accidentally stepped on the head of another and an argument broke out. In the ensuing fight, the hunter caught all of them as they were unable to hold the net aloft for one another. In their hour of need they all forgot about unity and therefore the hunter was successful in catching them.

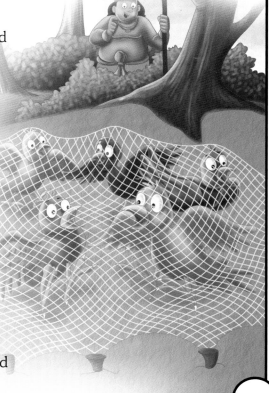

14 The King with One Grey Hair

Many moons ago the Bodhisattva, the Enlightened being, was born as King Makhadeva. The king had already lived for eighty-four years and had many more years to live, when one day his royal barber spotted a grey strand of hair on his head. Realising that he was growing old, Makhadeva regretted all the years he had squandered on worldly pleasures. Hereafter, he stepped aside and anointed his eldest son the new king. When his subjects heard about his decision they rushed to him. "Oh dear King, why do you want to leave us?" they cried. The king smiled and holding up his grey strand of hair said, "My dear subjects, God has sent the message that death is nearing. All my life I thought about wealth and power but now I want to get rid of my ignorance by meditating."

15 The Green Wood Gatherer

One day some students of a holy man went into the woods to gather firewood. One of the students noticed a tree which had no leaves. Thinking he had nothing much to do and could break a few branches while going back, he dozed off to sleep. In the evening, when he woke up he found that the branches were actualy green and not dry as he had thought. So, he returned with the green wood. Next morning the cook used the same to make breakfast for the students, but it took a long time to light the fire. The students got delayed for an important journey to a remote village. When the teacher got to know the reason for the delay he said wisely, "Don't put off for tomorrow what you can do today. A lazy person who does so puts others into trouble."

16 The Sacrifice of Vessantara

Vessantara was famous for his sacrifices from a very young age. He had a white elephant named Pacchaya who had supernatural powers to evoke the rain gods. Vessantara donated his elephant to the king of Kalinga when his kingdom was facing drought. So his king exiled him to the forest of Vankagiri. His wife and children too accompanied him. On the way Vessantara gave his chariot to four Brahmins and walked the rest of the way. One day a Brahmin named Jujaka paid a visit to Vessantara at his hermitage in the Vankagiri forest and begged for his two sons. Reluctantly, Vessantara gave them away to the Brahmin. Hearing of Vessantara's sacrifice, Sakka, the king of gods, decided to test Vessantara. He disguised himself as a beggar and went to visit him. He begged him for his wife to which Vessantara agreed. Such was the magnanimity of his soul! Impressed, Sakka revealed his true identity. With his blessings Vessantara got back everything he had sacrificed.

17 Grandma's Beloved

Once there lived an old woman who had a black calf. She loved the calf very dearly. Such was the love between them that everybody started calling it 'Grandma's Beloved'. The calf grew up into a strong bull and decided to earn some money for his old mistress. He went out looking for a job. and met a merchant who was stranded on the shore as his bullocks were unable to pull the carts across the river. The merchant went up to Grandma's Beloved and said, "If you help in pulling my carts I promise to give you two gold coins." The bull agreed and pulled all the five hundred carts across. After the job was done, the merchant put the two gold coins in a small bag and tied it around the bull's neck. Taking his hard-earned money, the bull returned home happily to give his mistress a pleasant surprise.

18 The Monkey and the Crocodile

One day Mama Crocodile asked her son, "Son, I have heard that the heart of a monkey is very tasty. I would love to taste one. Can you bring me the heart of the monkey who lives in the tree on the riverbank?" The crocodile thought for long and devised a plan. He went to the shore and called out, "Hello, friend! The fruits of the trees on the island are ripe. If you want I can take you there." The monkey's mouth watered. He sprang on the crocodile's back and off they went towards the island. After covering some distance, the crocodile blurted out, "Ha! Ha! My friend, my mother wants to eat your heart and I am taking you to her." The monkey got frightened but tried to keep his cool. "Oh, you should have told me earlier. I left my heart in the tree. You'll have to take me back to get it," said the quick-witted monkey. The foolish crocodile believed the monkey's words and started back towards the riverbank. No sooner than he reached there, the monkey jumped onto the shore, and capered up the tree to safety.

19 Coronation of an Owl

When the world was created all the creatures flocked with their fellow members to choose their respective kings. The human beings chose a gracious deserving young man as their king, the animals chose the mighty lion as their leader and the fish too unanimously chose the large fish named Ananda as their king. Likewise birds also gathered to make a choice of their king. At first they chose the owl as their king. Twice they recited, "Today at this auspicious hour we choose Owl as our king." But as soon as they were about to say it for the final time a crow interrupted. "Why should a grumpy owl be a king when so many younger and wiser crows are around?" protested he and flew away. The birds too felt that the crow was right and therefore decided to choose Swan as their king. Since then the crow and the owl are at loggerheads.

20 The Buck and the Doe

There lived a lovely doe with soft reddish brown fur, a fluffy white tail and wide bright eyes. One day she was grazing in the forest when a young mountain buck saw her and fell in love with her. He started following the doe wherever she went and showered her with praise about her beauty. There was a group of fairies in the forest who watched them secretly. One night the buck followed the doe to the village despite being warned of the possible dangers. But the love-struck buck didn't pay any heed. After walking a few steps, the doe sensed that a man was hiding ahead. Fearing that there could be a trap nearby she let the buck go first. There was a trap, indeed, and the hunter killed the buck. All the fairies accused the doe of his death, but the wisest among them remarked, "It was his infatuation that killed him. Infatuation gives one a false feeling of happiness at first but in the end leads to destruction."

21 The Mighty Fish

A long time ago in a lake in Jetavana, lived a kind pious fish who always thought about others' well-being. Once there was a terrible drought. The lake dried up and many water creatures lost their lives. Some, like the pious fish, lay buried under the mud but they became easy prey for birds and beasts. Seeing the overwhelming danger they were all facing, the pious fish decided to do something to save himself and the others. One day, ignoring all risks, he made his way through the mud and came up to the surface. There he performed the solemn act of Sacchakiriya or 'Act of Truth'. He called upon God Pajjuna and prayed, "O lord! Pardon our sins. Please send rain and relieve us from this misery." Such was his cry that it shook everything from hell to heaven and the god's heart filled with compassion. He sent heavy rains to the earth and thus the great fish and his companions were saved.

22 The Happy Man

Once a sage and his chief disciple were busy discussing some religious issues. While they were talking, the king, too, arrived there to pay his respect to the sage. But the chief disciple was so absorbed in his conversation with the sage that he failed to notice the king's arrival and did not greet him. Instead of the customary words of welcome, the king heard him saying "O, what a pleasure! What a pleasure!" The king took him to be greedy and thought he was expressing his joy after eating the royal dishes. He felt contempt for the disciple and loathed his presence. The guru however read his mind and revealed the disciple's true identity to the king. Formerly, the disciple used to be a monarch but had renounced everything for the life of a recluse. The "pleasure" the king had heard him talking about, was actually the pleasure of his life as a sage. The king realised his mistake and apologised.

23 The Beetle Who Challenged the Elephant

One day a dung beetle was buzzing across the rooms of a roadside inn when he spotted some empty liquor bottles on a table. He flew near the bottles and licked the few remaining drops and got drunk. Then, buzzing merrily, he returned to his heap of dung. Just then, an elephant was passing by the dung heap. He sniffed the dung and feeling disgusted by the foul smell, moved away. The beetle saw this and being under the effect of liquor imagined that the elephant was frightened of him. Forgetting the fact that he was just a small beetle he called after the elephant and challenged him to a fight. "Come on, you big fat fool! Let's fight and see who wins today," he shouted at the elephant. The latter, at first, didn't pay any heed, but the beetle, being overexcited, continued to jeer at him. At last the elephant lost his patience and threw some dung and water on the beetle, killing him instantly.

24 The Two Calves and the Piglet

One upon a time a household had two calves and a piglet. The owners of the house treated the piglet all too well and fed him with porridge made from the best rice. On the other hand, the two calves who toiled very hard in the field all through the day got to eat only grass and hay. The younger calf was very envious of the piglet. "Why should he get all the good food to eat when we do all the hard work?" she complained to the elder one. "Oh no," gasped the latter, "Never envy anyone because you don't know what price that creature may have to pay for his well-being. Very soon, the girl of this house will get married and the piglet will be killed for meat. It is for this purpose that he is being fed so well." Sure enough, within a few days the wedding took place and the piglet was killed, cooked and served as different types of dishes to the guests. Then the elder calf turned to the younger one and said, "My dear, now do you understand that our food is hundred times better than the rice porridge? It gives us better health and longer lives."

25 The Countryman and His City Wife

Once upon a time there was a famous teacher who taught in and around Varanasi. One of his students from the countryside fell in love with a girl from Varanasi and married her. But after his marriage the student became rather irregular in his classes. Once, when he went to attend his classes after a long absence, the teacher enquired the reason behind his long absence. The student heaved a sigh and confessed, "Guruji, my wife's behaviour is troubling me a lot. One day she behaves very well with me but again the next day she becomes rude." The teacher smiled and consoled his student saying, "Some people are born with such a nature. The days when your wife does something wrong, she stays polite but on other days, when she doesn't, she turns rude. Accept her the way she is." The student followed his advice and never again got upset by his wife's behaviour. After a while, his wife, too, realised her mistake and mended her ways.

26 The Groom Who Lost His Bride to the Stars

Once upon a time a rich family in Varanasi decided upon a date for holding the wedding of their son to a virtuous and pretty girl of a nearby village. Now, their family astrologer felt very insulted for not being consulted before fixing the wedding date and decided to take revenge. On the wedding day, the priest called the family together and warned them that it was the most unlucky day for the wedding and could lead to a unhappy marriage.

The family was terrified and called off the wedding for the time being. Meanwhile the bride's family married off their daughter to an honourable man of the same village. The next day when the family from Varanasi went to the village for the wedding they came to know that the girl had already got married. The villagers were very angry with them as they felt that a girl of their village had been shamed and they started a fight. Then a wise man came forward and said to the family, "Those faraway stars have no power unless we give it to them. You believed in them and lost the good fortune which could have come to you with the bride."

27 Lord Sakka and His Dog Mahakanha

In the reign of King Usinara, the people of the mortal world left the path of virtue and took to immoral ways. Sakka, the king of gods, decided to bring them back to the rightful path. He took the guise of a forester, and Matali, the heavenly charioteer, turned himself to a fierce black dog called Mahakanha. Together, they reached the gates of Usinara's kingdom. "Grrr…," roared the fierce dog as he approached the palace and his voice shook everyone from hell to heaven. Terrified, all the men fled into the city and shut the city gates. Sakka, disguised as the forester, said to the frightened king, "This dog is hungry and will devour all those who commit sins," and went on to explain the difference between sin and virtue. Finally, Sakka revealed his identity and returned to his heavenly abode. From then on, the king and his people left the wrongful path and took to truth and virtue.

28 Poison Dice

Once upon a time there lived two gamblers. One of them was good at heart whereas the other was dishonest. Whenever the latter sensed that he was about to lose a gamble, he used to swallow the dice thus stopping the game claiming that the dice had got lost. Once, noticing the trick, the other gambler vowed to teach

the dishonest man a lesson. Next day, he smeared the dice with poison before the game started. After a while, when the dishonest man began to lose out to his partner, he sneaked the dice into his mouth as usual. Immediately the poison took effect and he fell sick. But the other gambler was a kind person and nursed him back to health. "My friend, I just did this to teach you a lesson. Never ever deceive a friend," said the generous gambler. Since then the dishonest gambler mended his ways.

29 Buried Treasure

Once an old man buried all his earnings deep inside the forest as he didn't want it to fall into the wrong hands. Only his servant, Nanda, knew about it. After his death, Nanda promised to help his master's son find his inheritance. But when they reached the forest, Nanda felt all important as only he knew the whereabouts of the treasure and became hostile. The same thing happened again and again. At home Nanda would agree to help him but every time he reached the forest he refused to do so. Puzzled at his behaviour the son went to a wise man for advice. Hearing his problem the wise man said, "Your treasure lies there where Nanda stands and abuses you. Nanda is weak at heart. So, when he comes near his little area of power, he turns back on you."

30 The Merchant, the Ascetic and the Ram

Once, the Bodhisattva was born in a family of merchants. One day in the marketplace he saw an arrogant ascetic clad in a leather garment. The man put up the bearing of a saint and asked every living creature to bow to him and show respect. After a while the Bodhisattva noticed that a ram was lowering his head in front of the ascetic. The ascetic took it to be an expression of his respect for him. But the Bodhisattva knew that the ram was getting ready to attack as the ascetic was wearing a leather garment which he apparently didn't like. The Bodhisattva, who was witnessing the whole scene from a distance, tried to warn him. But before the ascetic could hear anything, the ram knocked him down. He lay groaning in pain and before long, breathed his last.

31 The Birth of a Banyan Tree

Once there were three friends—a crow, a monkey and an elephant. Often they had disagreements on many issues and could not decide whose opinion was right as they didn't know who was the most experienced among them. Once, they were resting under a big banyan tree when the monkey asked his friends, "What was the size of the banyan tree when you first saw it?" The elephant thought for a while and said, "When I was a baby, I used to rub my belly against its tender shoots. You can imagine how big it was then, looking at my size now." The monkey then turned to the crow and asked him what he had to say. "When I was young, there was a huge banyan tree a little away from here. I ate some berries from that banyan tree and then dropped a few seeds here. This tree grew up from those seeds," the crow said solemnly. Hearing him, the monkey at once stood up and said, "Aha! Friend, you're then the oldest among us because the first time I saw this tree it was just a seedling. So, from now on, Elephant and I shall listen to your opinions as you are oldest among us. Your experience will help us a lot. We just hope that you stay honest and just." The elephant too agreed with the monkey and from then on, the crow became the advisor of the two. The monkey and the elephant were also happy with their wise friend who, in fact, happened to be the Bodhisattva.

Contents

The Story of the Month: The Wise King Fruitful

The Story of the Month

The Wise King Fruitful

01 The Wise King Fruitful

Once the Bodhisattva was born to King Badfruit of Mithila and was named Fruitful. King Badfruit died before Fruitful was born and Poorfruit, the king's younger brother, usurped the kingdom. Sakka, the god of Heaven, helped the queen find the way to Campa and take shelter in the house of a wise man. Prince Fruitful grew up to become a handsome young man. By the time he was sixteen, he had mastered religion and literature and was a skilled warrior. One day, he decided to sail to Burma to make his fortune. On the eighth day at sea, there was a fierce storm and the ship began to sink. All the passengers except Fruitful panicked and began praying to God to save them. Meanwhile Fruitful soaked his clothes in oil, so that it would help him float on water, then jumped into the sea and swam with all his might in the direction of Mithila. The sea goddess, pleased with his undying spirit and courage and his quick thinking, took him in her arms, flew to Mithila and lay him down on a sacred stone in a mango garden.

Meanwhile, King Poorfruit died. The royal priest had a white horse set free and declared that the first person the horse would stop by, would be crowned king. The royal horse roamed for many days. At last, it reached the mango garden and stopped by Prince Fruitful. The priest, who had been following the horse, anointed the prince with holy water. Then Prince Fruitful was taken to the palace to Princess Sivali, King Poorfruit's daughter. She said, "Sir, my father had made a death wish. He had said that the future king would need to pass two tests. He will have to string a bow that can only be strung by a thousand men and he will have to find sixteen hidden treasures, the first of which is the treasure of the rising sun. Only then can he become king." Fruitful smiled calmly. He strung the bow effortlessly. For the second test, Prince Fruitful thought for a while. He remembered that the Silent Buddhas—the holy men who never preached, knowing that no one would understand their teachings were often compared to the glory of the sun. He guessed that the first treasure would be found where King Badfruit used to go to give alms to the Silent Buddhas. He went there and dug the ground and just as he had thought, found the first of the sixteen hidden treasures. Reasoning similarly, he found all the hidden treasures and thus passed both tests. Soon, Prince Fruitful was crowned king. He was married to Princess Sivali, amid joyous celebration all over the kingdom.

02 How the Turtle Saved His Life

Once a king built a pool in his courtyard for his young sons to play in. He ordered his men to put some fish into it. Quite by chance, the men also put in a turtle. The princes had not seen a turtle before and ran away in fright when they saw it. "Father! There's a demon in the lake," they complained. The king was very fond of his sons and he ordered his men to kill the turtle. But they did not know how to. After much discussion, an old man, who had always been afraid of the water, said, "Why don't you throw it into the water where it flows out over the rocks into the river. Then it will surely be killed." When the turtle heard this, he popped his head out of his shell and said, "Oh, please don't be so cruel as to throw me into the river!" The sentries thought that would be the best way to kill it and threw it into the water. The turtle laughed as he swam back home.

03 The Nymph and the Ascetic

Once Bodhisattva was born to a rich family. But he renounced all worldly pleasures and started leading the life of an ascetic. One morning, when he was bathing in the spring near his hermitage, a beautiful water nymph caught a glimpse of him and immediately fell in love. "Why is a young handsome man like him leading a life of hardships," wondered the nymph. "Probably he does not know there's so much pleasure in the world." She sang a beautiful song hoping that Bodhisattva would fall in love with her listening to her melodic voice. But he was unmoved. Surprised, the nymph went up to him and said, "O, my lord! Why are you ignoring all the pleasures of life and leading a life of hardship? You can take up meditation once you're old." Hearing this, the ascetic smiled and said, "My dear good lady, no one knows whether I will live that long." The nymph realised that she would never be able to move him and vanished forever.

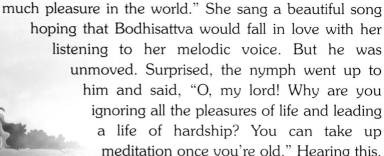

04 The Conqueror of Anger

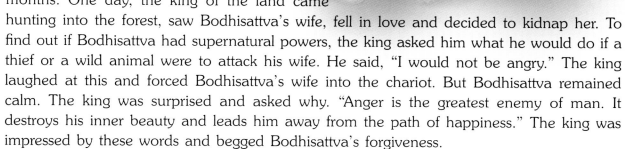

Once Bodhisattva, the Enlightened Being, was born into a highly educated family. When he reached his youth, he decided to renounce all worldly pleasures and lead the life of an ascetic. His wife too resolved to accompany him through all the hardships of an ascetic's life. They built a hut deep in a forest to stay for a few months. One day, the king of the land came hunting into the forest, saw Bodhisattva's wife, fell in love and decided to kidnap her. To find out if Bodhisattva had supernatural powers, the king asked him what he would do if a thief or a wild animal were to attack his wife. He said, "I would not be angry." The king laughed at this and forced Bodhisattva's wife into the chariot. But Bodhisattva remained calm. The king was surprised and asked why. "Anger is the greatest enemy of man. It destroys his inner beauty and leads him away from the path of happiness." The king was impressed by these words and begged Bodhisattva's forgiveness.

05 The Deer Who Played Truant

One day a doe brought her son to a wise teacher among the deer and told him, "O learned brother, please teach my little son the tricks to save himself from danger." The teacher agreed. From the next day, the little deer started taking lessons. Now, this little deer was very naughty. For the first few days he took his lessons attentively, but as the days passed, he became restless and was interested only in playing with the other deer. Soon, he began missing classes and learnt nothing of self-defence. One day, while playing, he stepped on a snare and got trapped. When this bad news reached his mother, she broke into tears. The teacher went up to her and said softly, "Dear sister, I feel sorry for what has happened to him. I tried my best to teach him self-defence. But he was not willing to learn. What could I possibly have taught him? A teacher can't do anything if the student is not willing to learn."

06 The Story of the Jealous Cousin

Buddha's popularity made Devadutta, his cunning first cousin, jealous. He thought of a way to lessen Buddha's popularity. He went to Magadha to meet its young crown prince, Ajatshatru, to persuade him to kill his father, Bimbisara. Bimbisara was one of the main supporters of Buddha. If Bimbisara were dead, Buddha's popularity would lessen. Devadutta even tried to kill Buddha. Once Devadutta hurled a stone at Buddha from the Gridhrakut Mountain, but, magically, two other stones came in its way and stopped it. Devadutta was dumbfounded. In yet another attempt, Devadutta set loose a rogue elephant at Rajgruhi where Buddha went for seeking alms. The elephant created chaos among the people. When Buddha came to the elephant, he gently touched the rogue on his forehead and instantly the elephant was calm. Devadutta was unsuccessful in his attempts. Eventually, people came to know about his evil plans and drove him out of town.

07 The Stolen Plough

One day a village trader kept his plough in his trader friend's house in the town and went on business. But the town trader sold the plough. When the village trader came back and asked for his plough, he said, "The mice have eaten up your plough." The village trader did not believe his friend, but he did not say anything. That evening he took his friend's son to another friend's house and left him there. When the boy's worried father asked after his son, the village trader just said, "A bird has flown away with your son." Knowing that his friend was lying, the town trader went to court and complained against him. The judge heard the father's complaint and demanded an explanation from the other. The village trader then narrated the tale of his plough. The judge understood everything and ordered the town trader to return his friend's plough and the other to bring back the child.

08 The Red-Bud Tree

It was early in spring when the eldest prince of a land went into the forest to see the Red-Bud tree that he had heard of so often. The tree was bare and wore a dead look and the prince could not understand why the tree was called Red-Bud. Later in the spring, the second son went into the jungle and he saw that the tree was covered with wonderful red buds. It was full of only green leaves when the third son saw the tree. Sometime later, the youngest prince went into the forest and saw that the tree was full of green pods. Returning from the forest, he ran to his brothers crying "I have seen the Red-Bud tree! It is full of green pods!" The other three princes shouted out how they had seen the tree. This resulted in an argument between the four brothers. The king, who had overheard everything, then explained to his sons that each of them had seen the same tree at different seasons.

09 A Fair Price

There was a king who had a young treasurer who was not fair in his dealings. Once, he gave a merchant only a cup of rice in exchange for his herd of horses. The merchant was not satisfied with the payment and thought of a way to get a fair price for his horses. First, he gave an expensive gift to the young treasurer. The next day, he went to the royal court, bowed to the king and said, "O Lord! I feel myself privileged to have sold my horses here. But, before I leave, I want to know the real value of one cup of rice." The king asked the treasurer to answer the merchant's question. The treasurer wanted to please the merchant and said, "Sir, a cup of rice is worth the whole kingdom of Benaras." The king was aghast. The king realised his mistake in appointing the young man as the treasurer. He made a new deal with the merchant for his herd of horses and banished the treasurer from his kingdom.

10 The Fearless Ascetic

Once a young sage was travelling with a caravan of merchants. The journey was long and the caravan halted for the night. Everyone went to sleep, except the sage. He was pacing up and down near the tents, when suddenly he saw some people emerge from the nearby bushes. They were robbers and they attacked the caravan with thunderous cries. The ascetic was prepared for attacks. Using a long stick, he fought the robbers alone. "You cowards can't even defeat one person. What will happen to you if I call my brothers?" said the ascetic. The robbers were stupefied at such strong resistance from an ascetic and they fled. Next morning, when the merchants found out what had happened, they thanked the sage profusely. "Weren't you scared of the robbers?" they asked. The ascetic smiled and said, "The sight of robbers causes fear to those who are rich. I am penniless, why should I be afraid?"

11 The Mulla Pleads Poverty

Mulla Nasruddin once borrowed a large sum of money from a money lender and failed to return it on time. The money lender went to the court and Mulla was brought before the judge. On being asked by the judge, Mulla admitted to have borrowed hundred dinars and promised to return it even if he had to sell his cow or his horse. Hearing him, the moneylender shouted out, "My Lord, He's lying. He doesn't have a horse or a cow. In fact, he doesn't even have food in the house to feed his wife and children". At this the Mulla smiled and said very wittily, "My Lord, if he knows that I'm so poor, doesn't he know that I am not in a position to return this money immediately".The judge heard the Mulla and dismissed the case.

12 The Mischievous Monkey

The Bodhisattva was once born a hermit. He lived in a leaf hut on a mountain and went everyday to the village to seek alms. A monkey would enter the hermit's hut when he would be away and eat all the food and make all sorts of mischief. One day, the hermit went out as usual to seek alms, but did not return for many days. The monkey came to the hermit's hut every day but found nothing to eat. So he went to the village to look for the hermit. The villagers had just performed puja and were about to offer the prasad to the hermit. "Let me also pretend to be holy and trick these villagers into giving me some food," the monkey thought. He went up to the hermit and stood near him, joining his forelegs as if he were in deep meditation. The villagers were pleased to see such devotion in a monkey and praised him highly. But the hermit recognised the mischievous monkey and told the villagers how the monkey troubled him every day. The angry villagers beat up the monkey and chased him away.

13 The Jackal and the Sage

Every night a wicked jackal went to a neighbouring village to steal all the delicious food items that he could find. One night the villagers laid a big net to trap whoever was plundering their village. When the jackal came to the village as usual, he fell into the trap. He somehow managed to escape and hid inside a cave. But the noise had woken up the villagers. In the morning when he awoke, he saw the villagers still searching for him. After a while, he saw a sage clad in simple clothes coming his way. In a piteous voice, the wicked animal cried, "Dear good man, I am injured. Please put me in your bag and carry me home." The holy man happily agreed and did as was asked. As soon as the jackal reached his den he cried aloud, "Here is the thief—the man with the bag!" and slid inside. The villagers came running and seeing the sage took him for the thief.

Thus the wise say, never trust anyone blindly.

14 Two Merchants and the Sacred Tree

Two merchants, Wise and Verywise, became business partners. They went to a distant land with caravans full of goods for sale. They made a huge profit after selling the goods and decided to share it. Verywise demanded twice Wise's share, arguing that his very name justified it. The two merchants decided to go to the Sacred Tree to seek its advice in resolving the matter. But Verywise was greedy and cunning and he wanted the larger share of the profits. He asked his father to hide in the hollow trunk of the Sacred Tree and pretend to be the spirit of the Sacred Tree. On the appointed day, Wise and Verywise met in front of the Sacred Tree. After the two had put forward their arguments to the Sacred Tree, Verywise's father said from inside the tree trunk, "Verywise deserves a double share of the profit." Sensing foul play, Wise set the tree on fire. Out came Verywise's father lamenting, "Better be wise than a cheat." The two merchants then shared the profits equally.

15 Heart of Gold

There once lived a rich man. He used to give a lot of alms to the poor and helped every needy person who came to his doorstep. Because of his charity and generosity, he was called "Heart of Gold." The gods in heaven were happy with the kind acts of this rich man. One day, Sakka, the king of the gods, remarked, "It's very easy for a rich man to be generous. What is praiseworthy is a poor man's generosity." The gods disguised themselves as thieves and robbed the rich man of his entire wealth. All that was left with him was a rope, a sickle and his nightshirt. One day, God Sakka disguised himself as a beggar, went to the rich man and begged for food. The rich man was eating the only piece of bread he had, but he gave it to the beggar. Seeing this, the gods decided to make him rich once again.

16 Prince Five-Weapons and Sticky-Hair

Once upon a time a son was born to a royal couple. The royal fortune-teller prophesied that the child would master the use of the five deadly weapons. The couple named the baby Five-Weapons and, in time, sent him to the best of teachers for his education. After the prince had learnt all that the teacher had to teach him, he started for the palace. On the way, he passed through a forest that was inhabited by a dreadful monster called Sticky-Hair. Sticky-Hair challenged Five-Weapons to a fight. But every weapon that the prince used got stuck in the monster's hair which was very sticky and matted. Finally, the prince himself got stuck to the monster's hair. Not losing courage, the witty prince fooled the monster saying, "Inside my belly, there's a weapon made of diamond which will cut through and kill you as soon as you devour me." Scared, Sticky-Hair set the prince free. The prince's intelligence saved him.

17 The Banyan Deer

In a forest lived two herds of deer, called the Banyan Deer and the Monkey Deer. The king of that country was very fond of deer meat and regularly hunted deer. To save the entire herd from being hunted, the leaders of Banyan Deer and Monkey Deer decided to send one deer to the king every day. The deer to be sent every day was chosen by draw of lots. One day, it was the turn of a deer among the Banyan Deer herd. This deer had a young baby. To save the baby from growing up motherless, the leader of the Banyan Deer went to the king instead of her. Now, the leader of the Banyan Deer was a very beautiful golden-coloured deer and the king had promised never to kill him. When the king saw the Banyan Deer he asked, "Why did you come, beautiful creature? The Banyan Deer then explained why he had come. The king was moved and promised to spare them all.

31

18 The Goat and the Panther

A goatherd was taking his goats up the mountain to graze. While the goats were climbing up the mountain, a young goat was left behind. As she was trying to catch up with the others, she noticed a panther hiding behind the bushes. The goat thought of a plan to save herself. She went to the panther and said, "Good day to you, Uncle. You've always been very nice to us. My mother too sends her greetings to you." The panther looked at her skeptically and said, "Do you think I'll let you go scot-free if you call me uncle?" The goat then pleaded for her life. But the panther took no pity on the goat and pounced on her. The poor goat could not outwit the panther with her wits.

19 The Hermit and the Elephant

A hermit once found a baby elephant in the forest. He brought the elephant calf to his hermitage and reared him like a child. As time passed, the hermit became very fond of the elephant and named him Somadatta. One day, the hermit brought a lot of bananas home, then left for the village. While he was away, Somadatta ate all the bananas out of greed. Soon, his stomach bloated and he died. When the hermit returned and found his beloved Somadatta dead, he wept bitterly, hugging the elephant's corpse. The Bodhisattva, a wise man, saw the hermit and said, "Don't lament. One who is born is sure to die. It's only your attachment which is the cause of your sorrow." The hermit realised the truth of his life and overcame his sorrow.

20 The Mouse Merchant

Once a man picked up a dead mouse hearing the royal advisor's remark that he could make a fortune out of it. He sold it to a shopkeeper who wanted it for his cat in exchange for a copper coin. The man bought some cakes with the coin and sold them to some flower pickers for a good price. He bought more cakes with the money and sold them. He kept doing that until he had made enough money to open a sweetshop. The sweetshop did good business and the man was able to buy a gold ring set with a ruby. He sold the ring to a merchant from a distant land for a huge sum of money. Then he gifted the royal advisor a thousand gold coins as a mark of gratitude. Seeing how hardworking the man was, the royal advisor gave his daughter in marriage to the man. He was now the son-in-law of the royal advisor. After the royal advisor's death, the king appointed the man as the next royal advisor and he no longer remained an ordinary man.

21 The Story of the Crows

There once lived a crow and his wife on a banyan tree near the sea shore. One day the two crows went bathing in the sea. "This is so nice," cheered the she-crow. The moment she uttered those words, a huge wave came and swept her away. "Oh! My dear wife has been washed away by the cruel waves," lamented the he-crow. Hearing him, the other crows came running and they started cawing together. An elderly crow suggested, "Let's empty the sea water and save her. We need not fear the sea as we are superior beings". So the crows started drawing out the sea water with their beaks, singing proudly:

Hehaw! Hehaw! We're the mighty lot
Can easily dry out the water of a sea or a pot
Let's save our beautiful friend
And set a heroic trend

Hearing their words, the sea spirit became angry and swept them all away with a huge sea wave.

22 The Story of Matanga

Matanga belonged to a low caste. People of the higher classes looked down upon him. One day, on his way home, he chanced upon Ditthamangalika, a beautiful maiden and her friends. The maidens, who were of a higher caste than Matanga, considered sighting him inauspicious and beat him up. Insulted, Matanga decided to protest and fight against the evil notion of caste. He began a hunger strike outside Ditthamangalika's house, demanding Ditthamangalika's hand in marriage. For seven days, he did not eat or drink anything and became very weak. Fearing Matanga's death in front of his house, Ditthimangalika's father agreed to the marriage. "I'm a human being, of flesh and blood, just like you. Then why do people like you despise me?" Matanga asked Ditthamangalika, after they had married. Ditthimangalika began to love and respect Matanga. Together, they spread the message of brotherhood and equality.

23 Demons in the Desert

There lived two friends, Sridhar and Shanidhar. Both of them were rich merchants. One day, they decided to go to a distant land to trade. On the way, there was the Waterless Desert. Demons lived there. Sridhar, being adventurous, opted to go first, thinking he would enjoy the better journey. Shanidhar agreed and let Sridhar go first, thinking that he would have the safer journey, as Sridhar and his men would clear the forest roads. On the way, Sridhar and his men had a difficult journey through the forest roads. In the Waterless Desert, demons, disguised as travellers, misled them and ate them. Some months later, Shanidhar started his journey. But he was wise enough to identify the demons and guard his men and himself against being misled and killed. So, they reached their destination safely and returned home happily.

24 How the Monkey Saved His Troop

A troop of monkeys lived on a hill close to a river. They used to eat the ripe mangoes of a tree on the riverbank. One day, the king went fishing to the river. He tasted a ripe mango from the tree. Finding it delicious, he decided to pluck all the mangoes on the tree the following day. But early next morning, the monkeys went to the tree to eat the mangoes. Their chatter woke up the king and he ordered his archers to shoot the monkeys. The chief of the monkeys heard the king's order and immediately thought of a way to save his troop and himself. He climbed up to a branch that hung over the water, walked to the tip of the branch and had every member of his troop jump off his back, one by one, to the hill across the river. All the monkeys reached their home in the hill safely. That is how the monkey saved his troop.

25 Great Gift and the Wish-Fulfilling Gem

The Bodhisattva was once born as a kind-hearted prince named Great Gift. One day the prince went to a nearby village and saw the sufferings of his poor subjects. Moved with pity, he offered them riches. But it wasn't enough to rid everybody's poverty. So he decided to get the Wish-fulfilling Gem for them and set out on a long voyage to the fountain on Jewel Island. But he was an unwelcome guest on the Jewel Island. The inhabitants did not welcome the prince, who was a stranger to them. But Prince Great Gift did not lose heart. He helped the king of the island to guard the castle where the Wish-fulfilling Gem was kept. Pleased with the prince's goodness and his services, the king gifted him the Wish-fulfilling Gem. The prince took it home and it brought everyone riches enough to fulfill their needs.

26 The Great Horse Knowing-One

The Bodhisattva once served the king of Benaras as a strong and wise horse. The king named him Great Knowing-One, for the horse could sense his rider's thoughts. Once, Benaras was attacked by seven neighbouring states. The bravest of the king's knights rode on Great Knowing-One to fight the enemies. Deciding to avoid bloodshed, Great Knowing-One suggested to the knight, "Sir Knight, let's not kill any of the enemy kings and instead capture them alive. I'll help you to do that." Saying so, Great Knowing-One stormed through the enemy cavalries. The knight captured the seven kings. But an enemy sword cut through Great Knowing-One's stomach and he bled to death. Before dying, the noble horse pleaded with his king to pardon the seven enemy kings. The king did as the horse wished and pardoned the kings and set them free. The enemy kings turned friends.

27 Interdependence

One day the trees in a forest were having a heated discussion. "All animals come to rest in our shade and dirty the place when they leave," said the fir tree. "We must teach them a lesson," cried the sal tree. "Calm down, my friends. If you drive away animals we can come to harm," explained the old banyan tree. But the other trees refused to listen to him and planned ways to drive away the animals. One day, when the animals were gathered under the shade as usual, the trees swayed so violently that the animals ran away in fright. The trees now felt happy and free from the noise created by the animals. However, the next day, two woodcutters approached the trees with their axes. One of them said to the other, "Finally these animals have stopped coming here. We can now peacefully cut the trees for wood." Saying this, they chopped up the sal tree while the surrounding trees watched helplessly.

28 Achieving Nothing

The Bodhisattva was an ascetic. He had five hundred followers, who lived with him in his mountain abode. One day, half of his followers, including the chief of the followers, were away looking for food. Suddenly, the Bodhisattva fell sick and took to bed. The followers who remained at the abode reached his bedside to tend to him. They asked him what his life's achievement was. The Bodhisattva replied, "Nothing." The followers failed to understand the true meaning of the wise man's words. They considered him to be a failure because he had achieved nothing. Soon after, the Bodhisattva died. The foolish followers gave him a simple burial, without any ceremony. When the chief of the followers returned, he explained to the others that their master had achieved such divinity that he could see beyond the ordinary appearance of things. But they did not understand him either. One night, the Bodhisattva appeared before his followers and said, "The one who hears the Truth and understands it immediately is far better off than a hundred fools who spend a hundred years thinking." The followers then realised that one should listen when the wise speak. They spent their lives in meditation and the search for Truth.

Contents

The Story of the Month: The Greedy Wife

The Story of the Month

The Greedy Wife

01 The Greedy Wife

One day a man and his wife were crossing the forest. Suddenly a group of bandits pounced on them. "Give us whatever money or jewels you have," demanded the leader of the group, "or else I shall slay your wife!" "I am poor and have no money!" pleaded the man. Now, the wife happened to be a very greedy person. Aware that bandits keep a lot of money, she at once turned to the leader and made up a story, "Oh please save me from my husband. He beats me and doesn't give me enough to eat!" she said entreatingly. The husband was appalled at his wife's treachery. The leader of the bandits took pity on the wife and killed the poor husband.

Satisfied with the turn of events, the greedy wife happily followed the group of bandits to their hideout. As soon as she reached there, she spotted bags full of precious jewels and gold coins! "Oh how I wish I could get those jewels and then lead a happy life with lots of clothes, food and riches!" she thought and then began working out a way to dupe the bandits and escape with the wealth.

It was late in the evening; the group of bandits had just finished their dinner and was getting ready to retire to their beds. The greedy wife took a glance at the bags. She waited patiently for the bandits to fall asleep. The leader of the group was about to go to bed when he noticed that the woman was still awake! Realising that something was wrong, he pretended to sleep.

As soon as she saw that everyone was fast asleep, the woman stealthily picked up a bag of jewels and turned to go. But lo, standing at the entrance was the leader with his big sword! "You lying and unfaithful woman! You made me kill your husband and now you are planning to escape with the jewels!" he shouted angrily. The greedy woman was speechless.

She had nothing to say in her defence. "You shall be rightly paid for your sins!" said the leader and took the woman to a cell.

On her way to the cell the woman noticed a jackal, which was about to eat a big piece of meat. But on noticing a fish swimming in the river nearby, the jackal turned its attention to it and forgot the piece of meat he had. He dived straight into the water to grab the fish, leaving his piece of meat on the bank. But alas! The fish wriggled away and the jackal had no choice but to return to the bank where he had left the meat. But no sooner had he swam out of the water than he saw an eagle flying away with the meat. The woman then understood how, like the jackal, she too had lost everything because of her greed.

02 The Antelope and the Hunter

An antelope had a favourite tree in the forest. He ate the fruits of the tree everyday. In the same area there was a hunter who trapped and killed animals regularly. The hunter soon discovered that while all the other animals ate fruits from all the trees of the forest, the antelope ate only from one particular tree. He soon came up with a plan to catch the antelope and placed some fruits below the tree as bait. He then kept the noose trap open and hid behind the branches of the tree. When the antelope arrived, he saw something strange—fruits lying strewn at the foot of his favourite tree. "How come there are so many fruits lying here today!" he wondered aloud. The antelope started examining the tree carefully and found the hunter hiding behind the branches! Pretending not to have seen him, the antelope cried aloud, "Since my favourite tree is behaving in a strange way, I will get fruits from another tree!" Saying this, the wise antelope ran away.

03 The Talkative Turtle

Once there lived in a river a turtle who just could not stop talking! One day, his friends, the two geese who lived near the river, came to bid him farewell. "Goodbye friend, we are going to fly away to a distant land!" they said. "Oh! please take me along!" pleaded the turtle. "But you cannot fly like us, so how can we take you along?" the geese asked. However, after thinking long and hard, they came up with a plan. The geese would hold the two ends of a stick while flying and make the turtle hold on to it with his mouth. However, they warned the turtle not to open his mouth. While the geese along with the turtle were flying over a village, a group of children, surprised by this unusual sight, cried out, "What a strange sight! Have you ever seen two birds carrying a turtle like that?" Angry at such a remark, the turtle opened his mouth to reply. But alas! He lost his grip, fell to the ground and died.

04 The Righteous King

The Bodhisattva was once the king of a very prosperous kingdom. However, as time passed, diseases, untimely deaths, floods and other calamities began plaguing his empire. The king became very worried and called an urgent meeting of his ministers and head priests. "Sir, we feel the gods are unhappy with us!" suggested a minister. "In that case we must organise a grand ritual and sacrifice a hundred lambs to appease them," declared the head priest. Everybody, except the king, at once welcomed this idea of a sacrificial ceremony. "I do not want to bring happiness to my kingdom by slaughtering animals!" the king protested. "But sir, as a king you must do everything possible to keep your subjects happy!" urged a minister. "I will not spill innocent blood for the sake of happiness, as that would mean committing a sin!" the king replied firmly. "Only with peace, love and a righteous rule will I appease the gods!" he declared. And rightly so, within a few days, the diseases and deaths ceased and peace and prosperity was once again restored to the kingdom.

05 The Monkey and the Snake Charmer

Once upon a time there lived a snake charmer who owned some snakes and a monkey. He earned his living by making the animals perform fascinating tricks and games. However, the man was very mean to his pets. He would beat them up and starve them for days. One night, after being spanked by his owner, the monkey ran away. The snake charmer continued to hold shows in various places but soon realised that people were not enjoying them without the monkey. So he went in search of the animal and one fine morning found him sitting high up on the branches of a tree. "Oh my dear pet, I have missed you so much! Let's go back home!" he cried. "Liar, you have come searching for me not out of love but because you've realised that without me your earnings have gone down!" snapped the monkey angrily. The snake charmer had to return home empty-handed, but learnt an important lesson that day—one needs to show love and respect to animals as well.

43

06 The Cunning Wolf

Once a group of travellers was crossing a dense forest. They felt very hungry after walking for some time. Aware that the trees around would not offer them anything edible besides fruits, the men decided to hunt some animals. Suddenly they saw a pack of wolves passing by. One of the men cried, "Why not kill one of these wolves and have it for dinner!" The other travelers agreed. So taking a club, the man went to the lake where the wolves had stopped to drink. He lay down on the bank, club in hand, pretending to be dead. Suspecting something fishy, the leader of the wolves decided to play a trick on the man. He stealthily walked up to him and tugged at his club. Fearing that the wolf would carry away his weapon, the man jumped up and pulled the club to himself. "Ha-ha-ha!" laughed the wolf and said, "I knew you weren't dead, otherwise you would not have sat up when I tried to take your club!"

07 The Miserly Father

Once there lived a Brahmin named Adinnapubbaka who was known to be a great miser. His sixteen-year-old son, Mattakundali, came down with severe jaundice, but his father, as usual, was reluctant to spend money on a physician. Adinnapubbaka tried to treat the boy on his own and gave him medication. But the boy's condition grew worse and there was no hope of recovery. When the boy was almost dead, the father laid him on the terrace so that all those who came to see the dying youth would get to see the father's wealth. Buddha saw the poor boy and out of compassion came up to him. He recited beautiful religious sermons to the dying boy and the latter, in his last moments, felt deep faith in Buddha's teachings. After his death he attained a new life among the gods. Since his death his bereaved father would go to the funeral ground and weep pitiably sitting by his son's ashes. Seeing this, Sakka, the king of gods, appeared before him and admonished him for his misdeeds. The repentant father then gave up grieving and started learning sermons from Buddha to make up for his sins.

08 Sutasoma

One day Prince Sutasoma was learning religious sermons from a pious sage named Nanda in his royal garden. Suddenly, a ferocious cannibal named Kalmasapasada, his son and a lioness entered the garden and abducted the prince. Instead of being frightened at being abducted, Sutasoma was sad because he couldn't offer anything to the hermit for teaching him so much. Hearing the prince express his regret, Kalmasapasada took him back to the ascetic who returned after having offered the sage something. Surprised at his return, Kalmasapasada said, "You're truthful, no doubt, but not wise." The prince smiled and said, "You are wrong, my friend. I am wise enough to know that falsehood makes a man lose eternal bliss and leads to suffering." Impressed with the prince's words, Kalmasapasada offered to release him but the prince refused the favour. "How can you set me free when you yourself are a slave to your cruel instincts and unhappy fate?" asked Sutasoma. His words stirred the cannibal's heart. He released Sutasoma and started leading a virtuous life.

09 The Quail and the Elephant

One day a wicked elephant trampled some young quails with his large feet without feeling any pity for them. The bereaved mother decided to kill the elephant before he could do more harm. So she made a plan along with her close friends—a crow, a fly and a frog. A few days later, the crow, according to plan, attacked the elephant and pecked out both his eyes. The fly then dropped some insect eggs on the wounds and soon the elephant's wounds were covered with maggots. In terrible pain the elephant groped his way through the jungle till he was overcome with thirst. He wandered about looking for water when he heard a frog croaking from the top of a mountain. The elephant, thinking there must be a water body nearby, went in the direction of the sound. The frog then climbed down the mountain and started croaking near a precipice. The elephant too changed his direction and moved towards the precipice. He stepped over the edge, fell to the bottom of the mountain and died instantly.

10 The Wisdom of Vidhura

Vidhurapandita was the wise minister of King Dhananjaya, the pious ruler of the kingdom of Kuru. Once the king had invited Sakka, the king of gods, Varuna, the king of snakes and Venateyya, the king of *garudas*, the large golden eagles, to his palace. They were discussing different matters concerning the universe, when all at once they started arguing as to who among the four kings was the most virtuous. Seeing that their argument was leading nowhere, they at last asked Vidhurapandita to decide who was the most pious. Taking care not to annoy anyone, the minister said, "O great souls of the universe. I am not the right person to decide who among you is the most pious. To me, all four of you are equal, like the spokes of the same wheel." The reply pleased them all. Thus Vidhurapandita resolved the argument with his good sense.

11 How God Saved Virtuous Vidhura

Queen Vimala and King Varuna, the ruler of the nagas had a beautiful daughter named Irandati. On hearing about wise Vidhurapandita, Queen Vimala desired to have his heart. Around the same time, Punnaka, the general of the *yakshas* fell in love with Princess Irandati and went to King Varuna to ask for her hand. King Varuna agreed to give princess Irandati's hand if he brought Vidhurapandita's heart. So Punnaka went to King Dhananjaya's court and challenged him to a game of dice. King Dhananjaya betted his minister Vidhurapandita in the game. But unfortunately he lost and Punnaka took Vidhurapandita to a secluded place in order to kill him with his sword. But his sword broke at the will of Sakka, the king of gods, who wanted to make sure that Vidhurapandita was safe. Punnaka realised that he was committing a sin and set Vidhurapandita free. King Varuna and his queen too realised their mistake and sought Vidhura's forgiveness.

12 The Fortunate Fish

One day a royal advisor saw a big handsome fish following his beautiful fish wife. He was so entranced by his wife's beauty that he did not notice a net that was cast ahead to trap them and got trapped while his wife swam away to safety. The fish was so blinded by her beauty that even when thrown on the shore, the fish went on lamenting for his wife. The advisor took the fish from the fisherman and said to him, "It seems you have not learnt your lesson. Your blind desire for your wife has brought you close to death but you don't seem to realise it. Had I not been here you would have been killed by now." The fish realised his weakness and thanked the wise man for his words. The advisor then released him back into the water and went on his way.

13 The Generous Merchant

The Bodhisattva was once born in Benaras as a wealthy merchant named Sankhasetthi. Once his friend, Piliyasetthi lost all his wealth and sought Sankhasetthi's help. Sankhasetthi gave him half of his possessions. Piliyasetthi left promising to help his friend in need. Some years later, Sankhasetthi lost his wealth. Remembering his friend's words he went to him for assistance. But Piliyasetthi was ungrateful and refused to help him in any way. When Sankhasetthi was coming back from his friend's house, his former servant whom he had given away to Piliyasetthi, recognised him. This servant knew about Piliyasetthi's promise. So, when he heard about the refusal, he brought Piliyasetthi's ingratitude to the king's notice. The king sorted out the problem and said that all of Piliyasetthi's wealth should be handed over to Sankhasetthi. But honest as he was, Sankhasetthi only wanted that much back which he had given to Piliyasetthi in his days of prosperity.

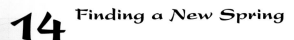

14 Finding a New Spring

Once a merchant leading a caravan to another country for trade lost his way in the middle of the desert. After a whole day of walking he and his men again came back to the place from where they had started. When everyone realised that they were lost they gave up all hope as there was not much water left and death seemed near. But the leader kept his cool. He said to himself, "I can't lose my mind. I have to think fast so as to escape this danger," and he started pacing up and down. Suddenly he noticed a few clumps of grass. "There can't be grass without water," he thought and asked the young men of the caravan to dig the spot. They dug and dug till their spade hit a stone. There was no sign of water. But the leader did not give up. He put his ears on the stone and heard a gurgling sound. Then he took a hammer and with all his might struck the stone. And lo! The stone split and water came gushing out.

15 The Hunter Who Killed the Monkeys

Once the Bodhisattva was born as a monkey named Nandiya. His mother was old and blind. Nandiya was a dutiful son and lived with his mother in a banyan tree in a forest near the village. One day, a hunter entered the forest to hunt. He was a cruel man and his teacher had warned him of dire consequences if he did not mend his ways, but the man would not listen. In the forest, he spotted the helpless old mother monkey and wanted to kill her. Her son, seeing his evil intention, came in the way of the hunter. "Don't kill my helpless mother. She can't even move away to save herself. Spare her life and take mine instead," he pleaded. "You fool! You're young. Why did you have to come in the way? Now both you and your mother will die," chuckled the hunter and killed them both. But on his way back home, he heard that lightning had hit his house and all of his family were killed. God had punished him for the sin he committed by killing the monkeys.

16 The Flies Who Showed Their Gratitude

Once the Bodhisattva was born as a winemaker. He was very kind and compassionate to all living beings. When he used to make wine, many flies, attracted by its fragrance, would fall into it and nearly drown. But he used to carefully pick them up, dry them in ashes and once they were fit enough to fly, he would release them. So the flies were very thankful towards him. This continued for many years. One day, someone lodged a false complaint against him and he was arrested and sentenced for some wrongful act that he did not commit. When the judge was about to write down his punishment on paper, thousands of flies flew towards him and moved the pen from his hand so that he could not write. The judge was amazed at this miracle and ordered fresh investigation into the case. Finally, the winemaker was proved innocent and was released. Such was this man's virtue that the flies showed their gratitude towards him by thus saving his life.

17 The Jewelled Serpent

Once, Nagraj, the king of the serpents, disguised himself as a human being and visited the hermitage of a sage. The hermit welcomed him warmly and soon they became very close friends. Since then, Nagraj became a frequent visitor to his place. But one day Nagraj visited him in his original form and this scared the hermit so much that he fell sick. "If you want to avoid Nagraj then ask for his dearest possession and he is sure to go away for ever," advised the sage's friend. Next day, when Nagraj arrived, the sage asked for the wish-fulfilling gem that Nagraj carried on his head. He kept pleading for it until one day Nagraj, getting irritated, said, "You ask too much from me, so I shall never come to you again." Nagraj never came back, but the hermit started missing him. Then the wise friend told him, "By begging for the gem you've made yourself hateful in his eyes, so he will never return." The ascetic realised that there was no point longing for his serpent friend and went back to his ascetic life.

18 The Story of Moggallana

Once there lived a man called Moggallana. He had a beautiful wife whom he loved very much. But this lady had a wicked nature and used to ill-treat Moggallana's old, blind parents. She kept pressing Mogollana to send his parents away to the forest. Unwilling to displease his wife, Moggallana one day took his parents to the forest and left them there. "We are unable to take care of ourselves. Please don't leave us all alone in the forest," pleaded his mother. But Moggallana paid no heed to his mother's pleas and went away. On the way, he fell into a pit and broke his legs. Unable to move, Moggallana lay there in pain. The Bodhisattva was passing by the pit. When he saw Moggallana, he helped him out. But alas! Moggallana had become a cripple for life. He then realised that one always pays for one's misdeeds and sought his parents' forgiveness.

19 The Brahmin Who Lost His Spell

Once upon a time a young Brahmin learned a magic spell from a wise Chandala, a person considered untouchable during those times. With this charm the Brahmin could grow delicious mangoes even out of season. Once during winter he exhibited his skill in front of the king and made delicious mangoes grow in the royal garden. The king was amazed to see the miracle and asked who had taught him the spell. The Brahmin did not want to acknowledge his humble teacher and so he said that he had learned the skill from a Brahmin in the city of Takkasila. But as soon as he said this, all his magic power deserted him. This shamed the youth and at the king's orders he went to his teacher to ask for forgiveness. But the teacher was deeply hurt and refused to accept as his student such an ungrateful man. The remorseful student then wandered away to the forest to atone for his sin.

20 The Tiger's Whisker

A lady once went to a wise hermit seeking help to win over her husband's love who she felt had become cold and aloof after returning from the war. The hermit agreed to help her with his magic potion but asked the lady to fetch a tiger's whisker to make the potion. The lady agreed and started visiting a tiger in the forest. Initially the tiger used to snarl at her, but as it got familiar, it became friendly and allowed her to come near it. One day, as the lady was caressing the tiger, she pulled a whisker off its face and ran to the hermit. The hermit took the whisker and threw it into the fire. "What have you done?" shouted the lady in amazement. The hermit smiled and said, "Look! Win over your husband's love the way you've won over the tiger's." The lady understood what the hermit meant and went home happily in the knowledge.

21 The King's White Elephant

Once some woodcutters nursed an extremely sick elephant back to health. The grateful elephant went back home and narrated the whole story to his son, who was strong and had a hide as white as snow. He said, "My son, as a sign of our gratitude we should always help these woodcutters. From tomorrow you'll accompany me and both of us shall offer our services to them." So the next day onwards, both the father and the son helped the woodcutters in their work. Sometimes they pulled up the trees; sometimes they would roll the logs down to the rivers; at other times they would fetch them their tools. In the evening, the white elephant played with the children of the woodcutters. One day, the king came to the forest and spotted the white elephant. He paid the woodcutters handsomely for the elephant and took him back with him to his kingdom. The king took utmost care of him and the elephant served the king as long as he lived.

22 Pieces of Gold

Two brothers were once sailing back home after amassing a large fortune from their various trades in foreign lands. The younger brother was a greedy fellow and replaced his elder brother's sack of gold coins with a sack of gravel. He planned to hide the coins and throw the other sack overboard. But by mistake he threw the sack of gold instead of the sack of gravel into the waters. The sea goddess watched over the bag and had a big fish swallow it. Later, the fish was caught and put up for sale. As luck would have it, the elder brother bought the fish and when his wife cut it open she got their sack of gold back. The sea goddess then visited him and told him the actual incident. The generous brother then gave half of the gold coins to his greedy brother who felt ashamed of his deeds and promised to follow the path of charity.

23 The Man with a Medicinal Plant

Once upon a time in Mithila, the Bodhisattva was born holding a medicinal plant in his hand and was thus named Mahosadha. At a young age Mahosadha became one of the chief counsellors of the king. Once, Mahosadha foiled the attempt of the king of Kampilla to invade Mithila. So the king of Kampilla took to other means to conquer Mithila. He invited King Videha to Kampilla and urged him to marry his beautiful daughter, Princess Pancalacandi. But Mahosadha could see through the king of Kampilla's trickery and to save his king, he dug out a tunnel leading from the royal palace of Kampilla to the River Ganga and reached the royal palace of Kampilla. He met King Videha there and revealing the king of Kampilla's plan, he took the king through the tunnel near the Ganges shore to meet Princess Pancalacandi whom Mahosadha had taken into confidence. There king Videha and Pancalacandi got married and escaped on a ship to Mithila.

24 A Rich Mouse

A rich merchant's wife was reborn as a mouse. She deeply loved the treasure she had in her previous life and so as a mouse, she dwelled close to the treasure which had belonged to her in her previous life. The Bodhisattva was then a stonecutter and used to work near the dwelling of the mouse. One day the mouse requested him to buy some meat for her. The Bodhisattva agreed and continued to bring her food for several days. One day a cat caught the mouse but she managed to free herself by promising her captor a portion of her daily food. Now the mouse had to share her food with the cat and so gradually she became pale as she could never have enough food for herself. The Bodhisattva, learning about her misery, put her inside a crystal box and asked her not to give food to the cat when he came. The cat came and on being refused any food by the mouse, jumped into the crystal box and was pierced to death. The mouse thus became free and in gratitude gave all her possessions to the Bodhisattva.

25 The Saintly Hare

The Bodhisattva was once born as a pious hare. One evening he was about to meditate when his eye caught the almost complete orb of the moon in the distant sky. He remembered that the coming day was the holy fifteenth day of the brighter half of the month—the day on which one should not eat anything before offering food to the guest. The Bodhisattva felt worried as he had no food that was good enough for a guest. After much thought, he decided to offer his body as food to anyone who may come to visit him. Now, Sakka, the king of gods, learning about Bodhisattva's resolve, appeared in the forest the next day to test his strength of character. He took the guise of a Brahmin and pretended to be in dire need of food. The Bodhisattva then lit a fire by striking two stones and jumped into the raging flames. Sakka was stunned by this act of sacrifice. The hare's soul went up to Heaven and Sakka, in his honour, adorned the moon with the hare's image.

26 The Ancient Mariner

Once upon a time there was an expert mariner named Supparaka who was wounded and became blind while trying to save his ship from a terrible storm. But he was gifted with many talents and was soon employed as the valuer in the king's court. Though blind, the man had an extraordinary ability to judge everything by his touch and to set a proper price for it. But the king never paid him well for his work. So, one day the mariner, unhappy with his low pay thought, "I should go and seek my fortune somewhere else," and left the king's service to look for a fresh living. Soon some merchants asked him to be the captain of their ship because they had a high regard for his judgment. After initial hesitation, the mariner finally accepted the offer and set sail for a foreign land. But after seven days of smooth sailing, the ship was caught in a storm. The mariner tried his best to save the ship, but in vain. When he found that the ship was sinking, he performed Sacchkiriya, the act of truth, saying that if he was truly righteous then his ship should be saved. The sea god was pleased with him and next day the ship reached its destination safely.

27 The Son Who Wished His Father a Long Life

Once, while traveling, a father and his son halted at a deserted house for the night. This house was haunted by a *yaksha* or spirit who had got a boon from Vessavana, the king of yakshas that if a night's guest sneezed and his partner forgot to wish him long life then he would be allowed to eat them both. It so happened that the father sneezed and the son did not wish him a long life. Immediately, they found the *yaksha* in front of them, about to eat them up. The son realised his mistake and started praying to God for saving his father's life. "O Almighty! If ever I have expressed my devotion to you then please save my dear old father," he cried. The father too, prayed likewise for his son and their love for each other proved so strong that the *yaksha* was unable to eat them.

28 The Poor Man Who Became Treasurer

Once the Bodhisattva was a spirit dwelling in a holy castor oil tree. One day a poor man came to pray to the tree. Since he was poor, he had nothing he could give the tree as an offering, except a piece of bread. So, when he saw others offering many expensive gifts to the tree, he thought that the tree would not receive a humble gift like his. He was about to go back when suddenly the Bodhisattva appeared before him and said, "My friend, I am hungry. Won't you give me the bread to eat?" The man was too astonished to speak and gave the bread to him. After eating it, the Bodhisattva said, "Dig the ground near the tree and you'll find a pitcher of gold coins." But the man did not take the money and instead informed the king about it. The king was pleased with the poor man's honesty and made him the royal treasurer.

29 The King's Promise

One day a king, on his routine rounds of his kingdom, came upon a childless couple. He was moved to see them suffering for want of an offspring. So he gave them his son to keep for a week. But at the end of the week, when it was time to get him back, the king found that the couple had fled his kingdom, taking the child with them. The king broke down and took to his bed. Seeing him so distressed, a wise counsellor, who was actually the Bodhisattva, arranged for a show at which the king watched a man swallowing swords. Amazed, the king asked his ministers whether there was any other feat more difficult than this. "O lord, promising a gift to someone and keeping it without regretting the decision are far more difficult than swallowing swords," said the Bodhisattva. The king realised the value of a promise made and finally accepted his loss.

30 The Lion and the Jackal

One day a jackal came to a mighty lion and bowing low said, "Lord! I would like to serve you as a servant." The lion accepted his proposal and made him a servant. He treated the jackal affectionately. The jackal, fed with sumptuous food, became very fat. One day, seeing his reflection in water the jackal thought, "I am as huge as the lion and by watching him I have learned all the skills of killing animals. So far, I have eaten the lion's leftovers, but today I'll kill an elephant myself." When he spoke about his plan to the lion the latter realised that the jackal was harbouring a false notion about himself and warned him about the danger of hunting an elephant. But the jackal paid no heed and went off to hunt. Imitating a lion, he roared loudly and jumped from a mountain top on to an elephant's back. But instead, he fell at the elephant's feet and the elephant crushed him to death.

31 The Story of Sage Agastya

Once a youth named Agastya left his family and took up the life of a sage. Such was his discipline and dedication that even Sakka, the king of gods, feared that Agastya might become as powerful as the gods. He put Agastya through various difficult situations either by making it impossible for him to have anything to eat or by appearing before him as a sage asking for alms and thus taking away whatever little food Agastya managed to gather. But Agastya never lost his temper. Pleased with him, Sakka offered to give him a boon. At this Agastya replied, "O almighty! If you really want to grant me a boon, then please don't appear to me in such splendour. I am making this request not out any pride but because I fear that your grandeur might distract me from my life of hardship." Hearing this Sakka blessed him and disappeared.

Contents

The Story of the Month: The Jealous Monk

The Jealous Monk

01 The Jealous Monk

In a village monastery there lived a monk. The rich man of the village supported the monk and he never had to beg for alms. Every day he was invited by the rich man to his house and served delicious food. Since he did not have to worry about his upkeep, the monk led a peaceful life following the right path and doing good deeds.

One day, an elderly monk who had followed the saintly path and became pure in spirit, came to the small village. His gentle manner and calm attitude impressed all. The villagers welcomed him with due respect and the rich man said, "O learned one, please oblige me by having a meal at my house. I'll make arrangements for your stay in the monastery." The monk humbly accepted the offer, went to the rich man's house and was served the most delicious meal. Afterwards the new monk went to the monastery and met the village monk. "Welcome, learned friend," said the village monk and took him to a room in the monastery. Later in the evening, the rich man paid a visit to the monastery with fruit juice, flowers and lamp oil and enquired about the new monk's comfort. "Revered One, I've learnt about the truth of life from you. You are indeed great," the rich man praised the new monk. He then invited both the monks for lunch to his house the next day.

Seeing the rich man's behaviour, the village monk was jealous and thought, "If this monk stays here, I'll lose my comfort and respect. I need to do something to send him away from the village." The village monk lost his peace of mind and kept thinking of a way to drive out the new monk. At night, before retiring to bed, the two monks met to greet each other, as was customary. While the new monk spoke warmly , the village monk remained silent as his mind was occupied with evil thoughts. The new monk went to his room and shut the door. He spent the whole night in meditation. Next morning, the village monk woke up early and left for the rich man's house without once meeting the new monk. As usual, the rich man gave him delicious food and enquired about his holy guest. "I've tried to wake him up. But it seems the tasty food that he ate last night at your place has made him lazy," said the village monk, trying to taint the new monk's reputation. The rich man then sent food for the new monk and asked the village monk to hand it to him. Burning with jealousy, the village monk threw the food into the fire and went back to the monastery. Meanwhile, the wise monk had sensed that the village monk was suffering from jealousy and had left the monastery while the village monk was away at the rich man's house. When the village monk returned, he found that the elderly monk had left the monastery. Realising his mistake, the village monk gave up all his worldly desires and prayed to God for forgiveness.

02 The Story of Mittavanda

Once a famous teacher of Benaras had a student named Mittavanda. He was very disobedient and never paid heed to his teacher's words. All he did during classes was eat and fight with his fellow students. His behaviour went from bad to worse and the teacher finally asked Mittavanda to leave his school. Mittavanda travelled for days and came to a small village.

There he earned his living as a labourer, married a poor woman and had two sons. Soon the villagers came to know that Mittavanda had been a student of a famous teacher. They started coming to seek his advice whenever they were in trouble. But here too, things did not turn out well for Mittavanda. The villagers soon found that ever since they started taking Mittavanda's advice, they had faced a lot of calamities. Their village was taxed, their houses got burnt in a fire and even the village pond dried up. "You're nothing but a curse," said the villagers and chased him away. On the way to a new village, Mittavanda's wife and sons were eaten by forest demons and poor Mittavanda was left alone.

03 The Disobedient Son

A merchant had a disobedient, irreligious son who was very unlike his charitable parents. Intending to rouse her son's interest in religion, the mother sent her son to listen to a saint's sermons in the temple one night, promising to give him a thousand rupees if he did so. The son, who was greedy for money, at once agreed. But instead of listening to the saint's teachings, he slept during the sermons. The next morning when he came home, he found that his mother had prepared a very delicious breakfast believing that her son would invite the saint home. But instead, the man took the thousand rupees and started making plans for moving overseas to trade. His mother pleaded him not to go but the man refused to listen to her. He packed up and left for the voyage. But alas! His ship met with a terrible storm on the way. It sank along with all passengers on board. Thus the son paid the price of disobedience.

04 The Vice of Pleasure

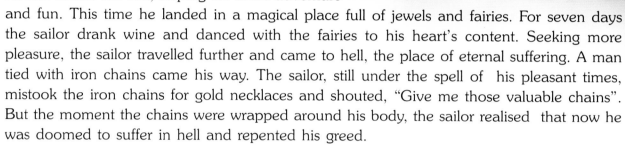

A sailor once went on a pleasure trip and reached a beautiful island full of delicious fruits and beautiful fairies. Having stayed there for seven days he went further on and came to an even more delightful land full of good food and wine. The sailor spent seven more days in that land and decided to go further across the sea, hoping for more adventure and fun. This time he landed in a magical place full of jewels and fairies. For seven days the sailor drank wine and danced with the fairies to his heart's content. Seeking more pleasure, the sailor travelled further and came to hell, the place of eternal suffering. A man tied with iron chains came his way. The sailor, still under the spell of his pleasant times, mistook the iron chains for gold necklaces and shouted, "Give me those valuable chains". But the moment the chains were wrapped around his body, the sailor realised that now he was doomed to suffer in hell and repented his greed.

05 The Partridge and the Crow

A crow was sitting on a coconut tree on the seashore. It was a fine sunny morning and the bird was resting for a while after having had a good breakfast. Suddenly his eyes fell on a partridge that was strutting on the sand. "Wow! What a wonderful gait the partridge has. I should also try to walk like that and be elegant," thought the crow and flew down from the tree. The crow walked behind the partridge for quite a distance trying to imitate her gait. Suddenly the partridge turned around and said, "Silly, why are you trying to walk like me? You are a crow and you should walk like a crow walks." But the crow refused to listen and continued to practice walking like the partridge. In his attempts to imitate the partridge, the crow soon forgot his own style of walking. But alas! Even after days of hard practice, the crow could not manage to imitate the partridge's gait properly and he could not walk like he used to walk before. Soon, he became a laughing stock.

06 The Talkative Minister

The king of Benaras had a very talkative minister. His nonstop talking irritated the king and he decided to do something about it. One day, while the king was sitting on the terrace of his palace he noticed a lame beggar sitting outside the palace gates. The beggar was cutting the leaves of the palm trees on the roadside into various shapes by throwing stones at them. Seeing the man's skill, an idea struck the king's mind. "Why don't I use the skills of this man to teach my minister a lesson?" thought the king and summoned the lame beggar. "You will have to use your skill to keep a talkative man's mouth shut. If you succeed I'll reward you suitably," said the king to the lame man. The next morning, according to the plan, when the king and his ministers were sitting in the court, the lame beggar hid behind the curtain. He filled a peashooter with half a peck of goat's dung and shot it at the talkative minister's mouth. The minister was startled and furious. The king then revealed to the minister his plan to teach him a lesson for his talkativeness and the minister realised his folly.

07 The Story of the Sarabha

The Bodhisattva was once born a Sarabha, a kind of forest deer with the strength of the lion and the wisdom of a man. The Sarabha was kind and compassionate. He would help every creature in need in the forest. One day, the king went hunting in the forest and spotted the Sarabha. He immediately took out his bow and arrow and took aim at the Sarabha. Seeing the king, the Sarabha ran with his utmost speed even though he had the strength to fight the king, as he had vowed to avoid violence. The king followed him on his horse. They went deep into the forest and came to a chasm which the Sarabha leapt across easily. But the king's horse could not leap over it and the king and his horse fell headlong into the chasm. The Sarabha saw this and feeling sorry for the king, pulled him out of the chasm. The king realised that the compassionate Sarabha was not an ordinary deer and with great respect sought the Sarabha's forgiveness.

08 Mahabodhi

The Bodhisattva was once born a wise scholar and was called Mahabodhi. He became an advisor to the king, who treated him with great respect. Seeing the honour that Mahabodhi received from the king, the other ministers became jealous. So, one day, finding the king alone in the garden, the jealous ministers approached him and said, "Your highness, you've been following Mahabodhi's advice and practising the kind of life he recommends. But what can a Brahmin know about politics and kingly duties?" The foolish king was easily convinced of the ministers' words and started ignoring Mahabodhi's advice from then on. Being an enlightened being, Mahabodhi could read the king's mind. When the king's dog barked at him one day, the scholar said, "This dog is imitating the disrespect you and your people show towards me." The king felt ashamed and sought Mahabodhi's forgiveness.

09 Chudapanthaka

Chudapanthaka, a young monk and his brother were the humble disciples of Sukhyamuni Buddha. While his brother could easily memorise verses, Chudapanthaka could hardly remember his guru's teachings. Seeing Chudapanthaka's futile attempts at memorising the verses, his brother once advised him to leave the monastery and return home. So Chudapanthaka sadly left the monastery. On his way home, he met Buddha who smiled at him and said, "Don't worry. You don't have to leave the monastery. Just stand outside the monastery with a rug and help the monks clean their feet." Chudapanthaka went back happily to the monastery and did as Buddha had advised him. As time passed, Chudapanthaka realised that he was indeed doing charity and helping others. This made him very happy and at last, he too, became Buddha's disciple.

10 The Flight of Sakka

In one of his many lives the Bodhisattva was born as Sakka, the king of gods. The demons once attacked the celestial kingdom with a huge army. Sakka boarded his golden chariot that was drawn by a thousand horses and marched ahead to fight the enemy. But the demons tolled heavy on the Gods. Seeing that they were losing the battle, the gods began to flee. When Matali, Sakka's charioteer, saw the gods fleeing, he too turned his chariot and flew up in the air. On the way, the wheels of the chariot almost crushed an eagle's nest with fledglings in it. Sakka saw this and immediately ordered Matali to turn the chariot around and move towards the battlefield. Seeing Sakka coming back, the demons thought that the king of the gods had come back with some new strategy and fell back in fear. Thus the gods won the battle.

11 Rahula, the Wise Stag

The Bodhisattva was once born as a stag. He was very wise and became the leader of a herd of stags. He had a nephew named Rahula, who was put under his care to learn the much-needed tricks that helped them to survive in the forest. Rahula was very obedient and followed his uncle's instructions diligently. One day, while the other deer were grazing in the forest, Rahula felt very thirsty and headed towards the lake which was a little distance away, unaware of a hunter's trap laid on the way. Suddenly he was caught in a net. "Help! Help!" shouted Rahula, but there was no one in sight. Suddenly, Rahula remembered the instructions given by his uncle. "Let me feign death, for a hunter never takes away a dead animal," thought Rahula and laid still, holding his breath. The hunter returned and when he saw Rahula, he mistook him to be dead and went away without him. Thus, by dint of his courage and intelligence, Rahula was saved.

12 The Golden Plate

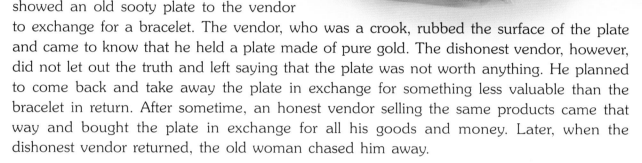

A poor old woman and her little granddaughter lived in a small town. One day, a vendor of pots, pans and handmade trinkets passed by their hut. The little girl pleaded with her grandmother to buy her a bracelet. Not having enough money, the old woman showed an old sooty plate to the vendor to exchange for a bracelet. The vendor, who was a crook, rubbed the surface of the plate and came to know that he held a plate made of pure gold. The dishonest vendor, however, did not let out the truth and left saying that the plate was not worth anything. He planned to come back and take away the plate in exchange for something less valuable than the bracelet in return. After sometime, an honest vendor selling the same products came that way and bought the plate in exchange for all his goods and money. Later, when the dishonest vendor returned, the old woman chased him away.

13 Poison in Honey

A merchant was passing through a forest with his caravan and attendants. "This forest is inhabited by demons. So be careful and don't pick up and eat anything lying on the ground without asking me first," the merchant warned his men. Gumbiya, the leader of the demons, was hiding behind the thick bushes and heard the merchant. He then went deep into the forest and strew the path with poisoned honeycombs. Soon the merchant and his men got tired due to the day's journey and decided to rest for a while. The merchant went away to fetch water from the lake. "Wow! Such delicious-looking honeycombs. Let's pick them up. The honey must be really sweet," exclaimed a few and picked up the honeycombs lying on the path. But alas, the moment they swallowed the honey, they choked and fell down dead. After a while, the merchant returned to find that his men had paid for their greed with their lives.

14 The Monster's Box

The Bodhisattva was once born as an ascetic. He had a monster as his disciple. The monster enjoyed listening to the Bodhisattva's teachings but never followed them. One day, the monster killed the attendants of a beautiful lady who was going to her parents' house through the forest. He made the lady his wife. But fearing that she would run away, the demon locked her up in a box. He used to swallow the box whenever he went out. One day, the demon spat out the box and went to bathe in the river, leaving the box on the shore. The lady managed to get out of the box. She met a young man who had a magic sword. Hoping to get rid of the demon, the lady hid the young man and his sword in the box with herself. After his bath, the monster swallowed the box again and went to listen to the Bodhisattva's teachings. As soon as the Bodhisattva saw the demon, he warned him that he was in danger. The demon immediately spat out the box and thus his life was saved. Then, as a mark of gratitude, the demon let the lady free at the Bodhisattva's bidding.

15 The Golden Goose

Once there lived a goose near a poor woman's hut. He had beautiful golden feathers. Noticing the old woman's poverty, the goose felt sad and decided to help. "I'll drop one of my golden feathers every other day at the poor woman's hut so that she can sell it and get money," thought the goose and flew to the hut. "I've nothing to offer you," said the woman when she saw the goose. The goose then told her about his plan. "Oh! Thank you, kind goose," said the woman and picked up the feather gladly. She sold the golden feather and bought food and clothes for herself and her two daughters. Often the goose came and dropped his golden feathers. This made the woman rich. But overcome with greed, the woman one day caught hold of the goose and plucked all his feathers. But alas! The feathers were no longer golden. The goose regained his feathers after sometime but never returned to help the woman. She once again became poor.

16 The Jealous King

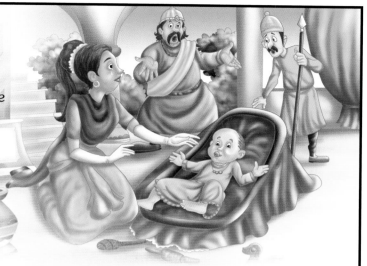

The Bodhisattva was once born into the royal family of Benaras. He was a beautiful baby and was adored by all. The queen loved her seven-month-old son immensely and spent the entire day playing with him and cuddling him. Day by day, the queen became more and more attached to her baby and had little time for her husband, the king. One day, while the queen was playing with her son, the king entered her room. The queen, busy with her baby, did not notice the king. "How dare you ignore me? I'm the lord of a mighty empire," the king shouted in anger. He summoned the royal executioner and asked him to kill the baby. The queen pleaded for mercy but to no avail. Blinded with jealousy, the king refused to listen to his queen. But, seeing the sweet boy the royal executioner was overcome with love and instead of killing him, left him in a hermitage in the forest. The baby grew up to be a saintly scholar and led a life of penance.

17 A Good Friend

A barber and a pious scholar were great friends. One day, they went on a journey across the seas. In the middle of the ocean the ship sank and the duo reached the shore by floating on a wooden plank. On the seashore, the barber hunted some wild beasts and prepared some roast for dinner. The pious scholar refused to have it and sat in deep meditation. Impressed with his devotion, the sea spirit appeared and offered to take him ashore on a huge ship carrying seven precious jewels. The scholar requested the sea spirit to take his friend too in the ship. But the sea spirit refused, saying that the barber had not led a life of penance and did not deserve to be saved. "All right, I then give all the benefit of my penance to my friend," said the scholar. The sea spirit then agreed to carry ashore the barber as well and the two friends reached home safely.

18 The Power of Faith

Everyday in the Jetavana Monastery, the Buddha used to preach his disciples. One day, a lay disciple of the Buddha was returning back from the village to the monastery. On the way, he had to cross a river. There was no ferry available at that time of the evening as all the ferrymen had gone to listen to the Buddha's teachings. "I cannot miss my teacher's teachings," thought the disciple and started walking through the river. He was so engrossed in his thoughts of the Buddha that he was unaware of the level of the water and kept walking as if he was walking through land. Suddenly, he got distracted and looking at the river water shouted out in fear," My God! I'm standing in the midst of the river." He once again closed his eyes and thought about the Buddha's teachings. And lo! He managed to walk across the river. He reached the monastery safely and narrated how his faith in his teacher's teachings had helped him to walk across the turbulent river.

19 Fear Maker and Little Archer

The Bodhisattva was once born as a dwarf who was learned, wise and skilled in archery. He was called Little Archer. Knowing well that his appearance would hinder him from getting a job with the king, Little Archer made a pact with a strongly built man called Fear Maker to seek employment as the king's archer while he would carry out the real work. They would then divide the pay equally among themselves. Things worked out as Little Archer had planned and Fear Maker became the king's chief archer. With Little Archer's advice, Fear Maker managed to kill a man-eating beast and a ravaging bull for the king. This earned him a lot of praise. But success made Fear Maker proud and he no longer heeded Little Archer or his advice. One day Fear Maker was asked to fight a large enemy army and he had to seek Little Archer's help who defeated the enemy easily and was suitably rewarded by the king. But he did not forget his friend and continued helping Fear Maker, who went back to his village.

20 The Proud Padanjali

Brahmadatta, the king of Benaras, had a very arrogant son named Padanjali who was good for nothing, except for idling around. This made Brahmadatta very worried. Prince Padanjali got into bad company and spent his time gambling and revelling. He believed he was wise and paid no heed to other peoples' words. Time passed, but the Prince's behaviour did not change. He knew that he was after all the prince and would one day be crowned the king. When the king died, Bodhisattva, who was the chief minister, decided to test Prince Padanjali before crowning him the king. He asked the prince to give an account of the duties and responsibilities of a ruler. The vain prince could not give a proper reply and mentioned nothing about the welfare of the people. It soon became known that he would be useless as a ruler and finally, Bodhisattva was made the king. Padanjali remained a good-for-nothing forever.

21 The Story of the Monkeys

Once when the royal priest was returning home through the royal garden, a monkey pooed on his head. The priest looked up and the monkeys jeered at him. "I'll make you pay heavily for your mischief," shouted the priest and left. Having heard the priest, the leader of the monkeys felt worried. He called all his fellows and warned them against the priest. While a few arrogant monkeys stayed behind, the others left. One day, a palace maid laid out some washed rice to dry. A sheep came along and started eating it. Annoyed, the maid threw a flaming log at the sheep. The sheep's fur caught fire and it ran into the royal elephants' shed. The shed, too, was soon swallowed up in flames and many royal elephants burned to death. Everyone considered this to be ominous for the kingdom. So the royal priest told the king that some monkeys should be sacrificed to clear away the ill effect of the unfortunate incident. And thus, the monkeys who had remained in the royal garden met their tragic end.

22 A Mother's Wise Advice

The kingdom of Benaras was once attacked by the king of Kosala. He killed the noble king of Benaras and made the queen his wife, but their son escaped unhurt through the sewage channel. Many loyal soldiers and officers of the late king joined the prince. Soon the prince gathered a huge army and decided to attack the cruel king of Kosala. The news reached the wise queen who was never in favour of violence. She sent a message to her son stating, "Close the city gates so that no food, water or firewood can enter the city. Tired with hunger and thirst, the citizens of Kosala will force their king to restore your father's kingdom." The prince followed his mother's advice and blocked the city gates. For seven days and seven nights nothing was allowed into the city as the prince and his huge army stood guard. Driven mad with hunger, the citizens attacked the unlawful king, beheaded him and made the rightful prince the king of Benaras.

23 Kandari, the Handsome King

The kingdom of Benaras was once ruled by a handsome king called Kandari who had a beautiful queen named Kinnara. One day, Kinnara saw a crippled beggar outside her window. The beggar was thin, dirty and bedraggled. But she wore a happy smile. The queen was attracted by the expression on the beggar's face and came up to her with a plate full of delicious food. "You're crippled and hungry, yet how do you manage to smile?" the queen asked her. "I'm happy because God has created me and blessed me with the gift of life," said the beggar. Her wisdom pleased the queen and she often went out to meet her. One day, the king followed the queen and saw her in the company of the beggar. Annoyed at leaving him and spending time with a beggar the king demanded an explanation. The queen smiled and replied, "Happiness and peace of mind." Then, listening to the beggar's simple words of wisdom, the king, too, felt ashamed of his sense of self-importance.

24 The Judge

A woman was once bathing in a river while her baby son slept on the bank. A demon saw the infant and with a mind to eat him, took the form of a woman and called out to the mother seeking to nurse the child for a while. The mother gladly agreed without suspecting anything wrong. After a while, the mother saw that the woman was running away and ran after her crying for help. "He's mine," shouted the demon and continued running. They went to the Buddha for judgment. Hearing their pleas, the Buddha asked the two women to hold the baby by his hands and legs and pull him hard. The one who managed to pull the baby towards her would be the rightful owner. While the demon used all his strength and pulled the baby, the real mother could not bear to see her baby in such pain and released her hold, weeping. Seeing this, the Buddha realised who the real mother was and chased away the demon.

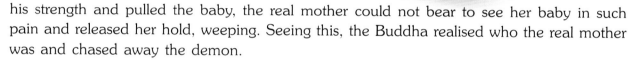

25 Truthfulness Pays

The Bodhisattva was once born as a quail and lived with his siblings in a nest. But unlike his brothers, the Bodhisattva refused to eat any worms or insects and fed only on twigs and grasses. As a result he was very weak and could not fly. One day, while his brothers were away looking for food, a fire broke out and spread rapidly all across the forest. All the animals, except the baby quail who was too weak to take flight, fled. As the fire closed in on the quail's nest and was about to engulf it, the baby quail cried, "O Mighty One, my wings are too weak to help me fly. All my brothers have left and I'm incapable of offering anything to a guest like you, except my frail body." At the baby quail's touching words, the fire took pity and decided to retreat, leaving the quail's nest unharmed.

26 Monks in a King's Pleasure Dome

An ascetic and his disciples lived in a hermitage nestled in a forest on the Himalayas. One rainy season, the disciples decided to go down to the nearest city and seek alms, while their teacher would stay behind to meditate. They reached the royal pleasure garden, where they sought shelter and food. They were welcomed inside as the king's guests and served a royal meal. The villagers, too, came forward and generously offered them alms. Later that day, the king offered them some good wine with dinner. Having taken wine for the first time, the monks got drunk and behaved improperly. Next morning they woke up and realised the folly of their action. "Let's go back to the forest to our master," muttered the monks and left for their hermitage. They confessed to their teacher how they had become slaves to worldly pleasure and promised never to stay away from him.

27 The Great Ape

The Bodhisattva was once born as a kind and virtuous ape. One day, a shepherd boy lost his way in the forest and climbed a tree to pluck some fruits. But the branch on which he stood broke and he fell right into a ditch. Moved with compassion, the ape pulled the boy out. Tired and exhausted, the ape went into a deep slumber. "Let me kill this ape and take home its flesh," thought the boy and tried to kill his rescuer with a huge stone. The stone missed its target but the ape woke up, shocked and hurt. He said to the ungrateful boy, "Remember my son, God always helps the benevolent as He has done right now." The shepherd felt ashamed and sought forgiveness. The generous ape forgave the shepherd and helped him find his way out of the forest.

28 The Falcon and the Quail

Once a falcon seized a quail and was about
to tear him apart when the quail, seeing
imminent death, cried, "Oh! Had I been with my
peers in our feeding ground I would never have been
caught." At this, the falcon, who was very proud of his
abilities, released the quail telling him that he would catch the
quail no matter where he went. The quail flew away and perched
on a rock. The falcon followed the quail and seeing it resting on the clod shouted, "Here I
come. Be ready to be my prey." Saying so, the falcon swooped down but the quail quickly
moved aside and the proud falcon smashed himself to death against the hard rock.

29 A Donkey in Lion Skin

A merchant went hawking from place to
place loading his goods on his donkey.
Whenever he halted, the merchant unloaded
the donkey, threw a lion skin over it and sent it
to graze in the nearby fields. Taking it to be a
lion, no one would dare go near it. One day, the
merchant let his donkey into a barley field with the
lion skin slung over it as usual. The villagers came running
with sticks and spears to chase away what they thought to be a lion. "Heehawww…" the
donkey brayed aloud in fear when he saw the villagers. Realising that it was actually a
donkey, the angry villagers mercilessly beat up the poor animal.

30 The Loyal Elephant

The king of Benaras had a she-elephant. She
was very strong and intelligent and was the
king's favourite. The elephant took pride in all
this attention and served her master to the best
of her abilities. Years passed by and as the elephant
became old, she lost her strength and could no longer
work as before. The king gave her away to the potter to drag his dung
cart. The elephant was heartbroken and sought the Bodhisattva's help
whom the king respected. The Bodhisattva spoke to the king and the king
realising the wrong he had done, once again treated the elephant well.

Contents

The Story of the Month: The Mystery of the Missing Necklace

The Story of the Month

The Mystery of
the Missing Necklace

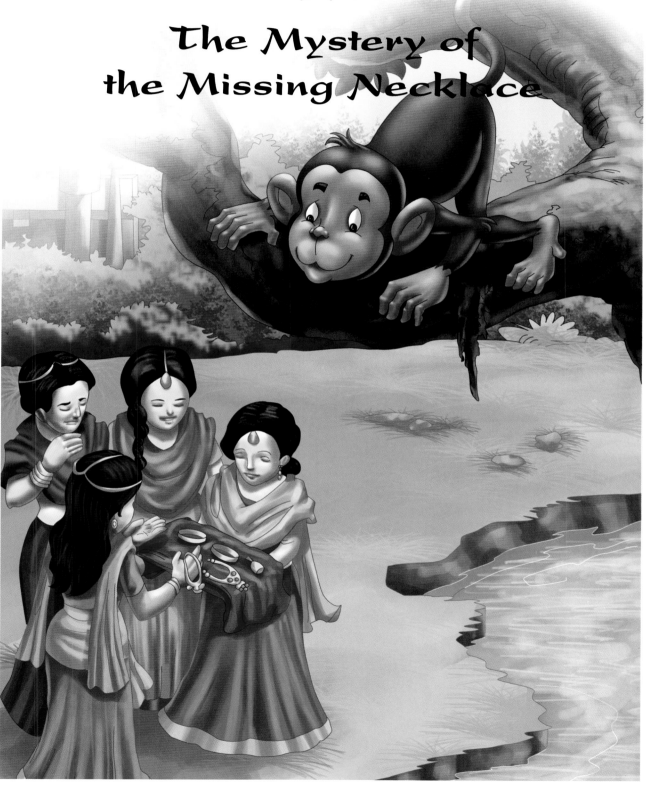

01 The Mystery of the Missing Necklace

One day the queens of King Brahmadatta wished to swim in the lake in his garden and left their jewellery with their servant girls before taking a dip in the water. Now, this garden was home to many monkeys. One she-monkey had been sitting on the branch. She got particularly interested in a beautiful pearl necklace that belonged to the chief queen. "Now I know why these queens always look so charming. If I wear that pearl necklace, then I shall look as beautiful as them," thought she and waited patiently for the right moment to steal the necklace. After a while, when the servant girl dozed off, the monkey swung down from the tree and grabbed the necklace in a flash and disappeared into the thick foliage of the tree. When the news of the theft reached the king, he ordered his guards to keep no stone unturned to catch the thief. Just then a poor man was passing by the garden. The hullabaloo from inside the garden scared him and he ran away. Seeing him run, the guards took him to be the thief and after chasing him for some distance they captured him. When he was produced before the king, he said he had stolen the necklace and added that the chief financial advisor had asked him to do so and that the necklace should be with him. When the chief financial advisor was questioned he passed the responsibility to the royal priest, who in turn passed it on to the chief court musician and he again involved the chief court dancer. But when the dancer was summoned to the court, she denied the allegation altogether. At the end of the day the king was confused and ordered all of them be put behind bars. Bodhisattva, who was at that time a minister to the king, didn't quite believe that these detainees were the actual culprit because the theft had taken place inside the heavily guarded garden and it was impossible for the poor man to enter the garden and steal. If he had not committed the crime in the first place, then there was no question of any others' involvement. "I am sure they are lying out of fear. The poor man must have involved the advisor to save himself. The advisor then must have involved the priest thinking that it would be easier for him if he involved someone very important. I believe the priest involved the musician thinking that if all were imprisoned then music could heal their pain and I am sure the musician felt the same thing when he involved the dancer," he thought and was quite confident that it was the work of a she-monkey. Then he ordered all female monkeys be captured and adorned them with imitation jewelleries. Then the monkeys were released by the king's men, who kept a close watch on them. Now, the actual culprit had hidden the necklace in a hollow in the tree. When her companions flaunted their set of jewellery with an air of pride, she could not hold her patience. To make them realize that hers was actually better necklace, she brought the necklace out and wore it around her neck. The guards noticed and scared the monkey to drop it. The queen got her necklace back and all the detainees were released from custody.

02 The Magic Priest and a Gang of Kidnappers

One day a priest was travelling to a faraway village along with his student when they were attacked by kidnappers. To set his teacher free, the student was asked to return to the village to get the ransom money. But before leaving, he warned his teacher not to use his magical power of bringing down precious jewel from the sky. Soon after the student left, night fell. The teacher, looking at the clear sky, thought to himself, "Why should I wait for my student and suffer like this when I have the power to free myself?" Then he implored the planets and uttered his magical words and down came the jewels, raining from the sky. The kidnappers who were stunned to see the shower of precious jewels, demanded more. But the priest could use his power only once a year. So when he failed to bring down more jewels, the engraged kidnappers killed him.

03 The Wise Goat

One sunny morning, when puffs of white clouds were gaily dancing in the sky, a little goat trotted up a high steep hillock to graze. As he happily munched on the grass, a crafty wolf came by the rock in search of his meal and his eyes fell upon the lone goat. His eyes glistened with greed and he smacked his lips thinking how delicious the goat would taste. He tried to climb the hillock, but at every attempt he slipped off. So he thought of a plan. He called out to the goat from the bottom of the hillock, "Hello dear goat! What are you doing there all alone? Come down into the field. The grass is sweeter here and you'll enjoy it all the more." But the goat knew that it was never wise to believe an enemy. So he smiled and said, "No thanks, my friend. I like the taste of this grass better."

04 The Ugly King

Bodhisattva was once born as the king. He was an ugly man. However, he was a pious and able ruler. His subjects loved him and wanted him to get married. Though a little hesitant at first because of his ugly looks, the king finally agreed to get married. His wife was a beautiful and charming lady. The king always hid his face, fearing his

wife might desert him if she saw how ugly he was. But soon his worst fears became true. One night, while he was sleeping, his wife entered his room with a candle and was terrified to see how ugly he was. She decided to leave him. The king was heartbroken because he loved his wife very much. Seeing him in distress, Sakka visited the queen and enlightened her with his teachings. "Your husband has the power and position to destroy you and your father's kingdom when you left him. But instead, he still cares about you. Look at the beauty of his soul and not just the face," he said. The queen realised her mistake and returned to her husband. The king was united with his love and was happy.

05 The Six Worthy Ways

Once upon a time there lived a rich man in Benaras who strongly believed that happiness and peace is more valuable than money and this he believed could be attained by leading a disciplined and virtuous life. The man wanted his little son to realise this. One day, while playing with his friend, the little boy accidentally broke an expensive glass elephant and started crying. Hearing him weep, his father rushed into the room and when he came to know the reason for his son's distress, he said, "Don't cry over a broken toy, my son. There are more valuable things in life like health, modesty, truthfulness and sincerity which makes a man complete. Rememeber never to lose these values else you will suffer." The boy always remembered his father's words and when he grew up, he was successful in every sphere of life.

06 The Sacrifice of Sivi

The Bodhisattva was once born as the pious King Sivi of Aritthapura. The stories of his kindness and charity spread to the faraway lands so much so that the gods in heaven also heard them. So Sakka the king of gods visited the king's court in the guise of a blind Brahmin. The king welcomed him warmly and enquired about the reason of his visit. "Oh! pious king, I have heard about your kindness and have thus come to seek your help. I really want to see this beautiful world with my own eyes. Will you please gift me your eyes?" The entire court was shocked to hear these words. But the king was calm and against the opposition of his friends and courtiers, he gifted his two beautiful eyes to the Brahmin. Sakka was moved by the king's sacrifice and revealed his identity. He then blessed the king profusely and returned his eyes.

07 The Story of Alcohol

One day a hunter named Sura noticed a strange tree where three branches spread out from a point on the trunk to form a cauldron-shaped hollow. Sometimes ripe fruits from nearby plum and pepper trees fell into the hollow. Whenever it rained the hollow got filled up with water. Sometimes parrots ate seeds of wild rice sitting on the branches of the tree and some of the seeds fell into the water. Then the heat of the sun fermented the water to form liquor. Seeing the birds drinking the liquid, the hunter wondered what on earth was it. Quite curious, he tasted it and immediately got intoxicated. When he recovered, he realised that he had accidentally learned the art of making strong liquor. So together with his friend, the hunter decided to take up winemaking as a profession. Soon their wine became famous in cities like Benaras and Kasi and people started drinking for pleasure.

08 King Sabamitta and Alcohol

Sura and Varuna, the two famous winemakers of Benaras, reached Savatthi to sell their wine. King Sabbamitta heard about their delicious wine and asked them to prepare it for him. The ingredients were mixed in two big jars and a cat was tied to each of the jars to keep the rats away. With time the brew fermented and began to overflow. The cats licked the drink that ran down the sides of the jars, got intoxicated and dozed off. The king's guards thought that the cats had died and the mixture was probably poisonous. They reported the incident to the king who thought that the winemakers had cheated and sentenced them to death. But later on when the cats woke up, the king realised that the drink was indeed  liquor and arranged for a grand wine-drinking ceremony. Sakka visited the king dressed as a Brahmin and enlightened him about the many vices that alcohol could lead a man into. Realising his mistake, the king prohibited drinking in his kingdom.

09 Monkeys Wearing Caps

Once a tired man carrying a bag full of colourful caps dozed off to sleep under the shade of a tree. When he woke up he saw that the tree above him was full of monkeys who were wearing his caps. He yelled at them and they screamed back at him. Realising that the monkeys were imitating him, the clever man took off his cap and threw it onto the ground. As he had expected, the monkeys imitated him and did the same. The man collected his caps quickly and went off. Fifty years later, his grandson passed by the same way with his bags of caps and rested under the same tree. When he woke up, he found some monkeys on the tree wearing his caps. Then he remembered his 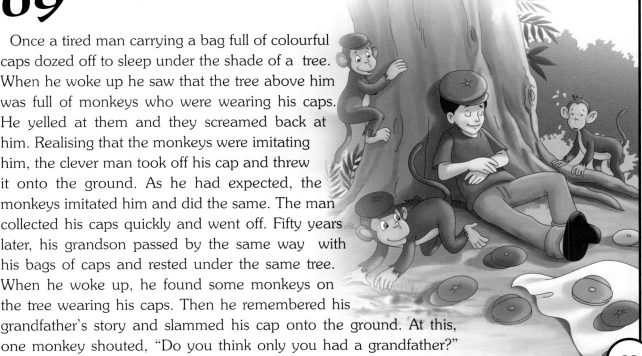 grandfather's story and slammed his cap onto the ground. At this, one monkey shouted, "Do you think only you had a grandfather?"

10 The Farmer and the Golden Crab

Bodhisattva was once born as a farmer. He became friends with a golden crab who lived in a nearby pond. Now there lived a crow couple on the tree near the pond. The she-crow wished to eat the farmer's eye and requested her husband to get a snake to bite him. The husband fulfilled her wish and had a snake bite the man. The man groaned in pain and became unconscious. The crab heard him and ran to see what the matter was. When he saw that the she-crow was about to pluck out the farmer's eyes, the crab caught hold of her with his claws. The snake came to the crow's rescue but the crab clasped him tight and made him suck the poison out from the man's body. When the farmer regained his senses, he thanked his friend profusely. The crab then crushed both the snake and the crow to death.

11 The Silly Kid

One day, a little boy climbed up on the roof of his house and looked across the frightening stretch of the jungle that was near his house. He was very scared of the jungle but had a hidden desire in his heart to brave a wild animal someday. It was daytime. The forest looked less menacing. He saw a wolf passing by his house. From the rooftop it did not look that fierce. The boy wanted to scare the animal away as he knew he was at a safe distance. So he screamed at it, "Hey! You ugly creature! How dare you to cross my home. Get off right away!" "I was just passing by," replied the wolf in a soft tone, realising that he was in the enemy territory. "Just passing by! Huh! Is this a thoroughfare? Get lost, I say!" shouted the boy. The boy was stunned at his own courage. But then the angry wolf growled back, "It is very easy to be brave from a safe distance. You are not brave at all. It's the height of the roof that has made you brave." He growled so loud that it frightened the boy and he ran back inside his house.

12 Ladyface

Once upon a time a king had an elephant who was very gentle and kind in nature. The king named him Ladyface. One night, some robbers gathered near the shed of the elephant and discussed their next robbery. They used rough, impolite language and spoke loudly about their violent ways. Ladyface heard them and got agitated. He became so wild in his ways that he killed his trainer. When this news reached the king, he was very worried. Now, the king had a wise minister who had a good understanding of animal behaviour. He went up to Ladyface and spoke kindly to him. Ladyface kept listening to him intently with his ears perked up. The minister sensed that something was wrong and learned about the presence of the robbers from the guards. He then decided to keep Ladyface under the care of some saints for some days thinking their pleasant words would soothe Ladyface and the ill effect of all the violent things he had heard would slowly wear off. The idea worked and Ladyface became gentler than before.

13 The Pious Asitabhu

A long time ago, the king of Benaras banished his son, Prince Brahmadatta, from his kingdom. The prince went to the Himalayas with his wife Asitabhu following him. They started living in a small hut in the midst of the jungle. One day, while wandering about in the jungle, Brahmadatta noticed a beautiful maiden and fell in love with her. Asitabu became heart broken at her husband's betrayal. She visited a sage who lived in the same forest to attain peace of mind. The sage gave her religious sermons which helped to calm her mind and she found happiness and comfort in the religious way of living. Under the guidance of the ascetic, she attained some supernatural powers and returned to her hut. In the meantime, Brahmadatta failed to make the beautiful maiden his wife and returned to Asitabhu. But when he returned, he found Asitabhu poised mid-air, lost in deep meditation. Though Brahmadatta requested her to stay on with him, she refused and left her home to embrace a religious life.

14 The Hawks and Their Friends

On an island, atop a big tree beside a lake, lived a hawk family. On the same island lived a lion, a turtle and a kingfisher who became very good friends. Once, after an unsuccessful hunt, some hunters decided to spend the night under the same tree where the hawks lived and seeing the baby hawks decided to have them for their meal. Hearing their deadly plan, the father hawk informed his friends about the danger. When both of them arrived at the spot, they saw one of the hunters climbing up the tree. The kingfisher sprinkled water on the fire while the turtle collected some mud and threw it on the fire to put it off. Meanwhile the lion came and roared aloud. Hearing the lion's roar, the hunters got scared and ran away, giving up their hopes of feasting on the baby hawks.

15 Khankhaak and Phya Thaen

Once upon a time, an intelligent son was born to the king and queen of Inthapattanakhon. Because the little boy was very ugly, he was named Khankhaak, meaning toad. When he came of age, he ascended the throne and proved to be a worthy king. Now, his popularity enraged Phya Thaen, the Rain God. "Always everyone is talking about that mortal king. I'll show him how powerful I am. I'll see what he does to save his subjects from my wrath," thought he and stopped sending rains to the earth. The long drought had a devastating effect and killed millions of creatures. Failing in all his attempts to appease Phya Thaen, Khankhaak organised a large army of humans, animals, demons and angels to fight the Rain God. After many days of perilous battle in heaven, Khankhaak won. He taught the Rain God how to be just and bestow rains on the universe seasonally. Phya Thaen realised his mistake and both of them became friends. Then after enjoying some days in Heaven, Khankhaak returned to Earth happily.

16 The Origin of Lake Nongkasae

Phya Khankhaak, after a victorious battle against the Rain God, returned to his kingdom to a grand welcome. Everyone in his court was eager to listen to the accounts of his days in Heaven. The king eagerly gave them a detailed account of the whole episode, from the day his army was organised to his battle with the Rain God. Later on, some people, after listening to Khankhaak's stories about his feats in Heaven, decided to retrace their way to it. They went to Heaven to learn all kinds of magical powers. After coming back to the earth, they tested their power against each other and eventually destroyed the whole earth. After the massacre, the piles of corpses laid together formed a huge mountain of dead bodies. A gigantic vine grew up from its foot to reach Heaven. Khankhaak shot the vine with his arrow, thus destroying it and everything around it, including himself. The root of the tree was destroyed and it left a large crater on the surface of the earth. Later on, the crater filled with water and became a lake named Nongkasae.

17 The Greedy Crow

Once there lived a white pigeon in a nest on the banyan tree. This tree happened to be near the kitchen of the king's palace. The cooks loved the pigeon very much and often, gave him grains to eat. The pigeon too liked the place and he enjoyed a happy life there. One day, a crow saw the pigeon getting food from the royal kitchen and mistook the grains to be some delicious royal food and his mouth watered at the thought of those exotic dishes. Intending to get a share of the pigeon's meal, the crow one day visited the pigeon's nest to offer his friendship. But, when he realised that all that the pigeon got from the royal kitchen were grains, he flew away and stealthily crept into the kitchen. He tried to get some meat from the cauldron. But, in the process he disturbed a ladle that created a big noise. The noise alerted the cook and he caught hold of the crow and killed him.

18 The Kind Buffalo

Once in a jungle there lived a kind buffalo. He was very virtuous and always upheld the value of good conduct and forbearance. In that forest there also lived a wicked monkey whose favourite pastime was to torture the buffalo one way or the other, either by twisting his tail or by swinging around holding his horns and so on. The buffalo was tired of his heartless pranks but never did he lose his patience. One day, a *yaksha* who also resided in the same forest told him "Why don't you just kill this silly monkey?" But the buffalo replied, "I'm patient because I know one day he will learn his lessons. Indeed, just as he had said, a few days later another buffalo came to the spot when the gentle one was not present. The monkey, mistaking him to be the same humble buffalo, jumped on him and yanked his ears. But this buffalo was not ready to take his silly pranks and threw him on to the ground and trampled him with his hooves.

19 The Dancing Peacock

King Golden Swan had a beautiful daughter. When she was of marriageable age, he invited all the birds to a gathering in his royal palace where the princess would choose her husband. When they all assembled at the court, the lovely princess looked at all of them and her eyes were drawn towards a gorgeous peacock with beautiful tail feathers. She chose the peacock to be her husband. On hearing this, the peacock was overwhelmed with joy and felt so proud that he broke into a wild dance of joy. He forgot all about being modest before the other guests. Everyone present there giggled at his behaviour. King Golden Swan was embarrassed to see that his daughter had chosen such an unworthy suitor who did not know proper conduct and was vainly proud. Addressing the peacock, the king said, "Sir, you're no doubt the most handsome bird but I can't allow my daughter to marry someone like you." The king then got his daughter married to his worthy nephew.

20 The Miserly Treasurer

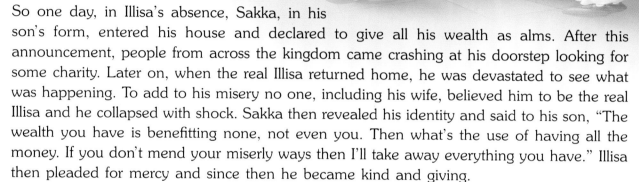

Once, there lived a treasurer named Illisa who was the worst miser anybody had ever known. His late father, who was loved by all for his kind ways, was reborn as Sakka, the king of gods. When Sakka saw the miserly ways of his son, he decided to teach him a lesson. So one day, in Illisa's absence, Sakka, in his son's form, entered his house and declared to give all his wealth as alms. After this announcement, people from across the kingdom came crashing at his doorstep looking for some charity. Later on, when the real Illisa returned home, he was devastated to see what was happening. To add to his misery no one, including his wife, believed him to be the real Illisa and he collapsed with shock. Sakka then revealed his identity and said to his son, "The wealth you have is benefitting none, not even you. Then what's the use of having all the money. If you don't mend your miserly ways then I'll take away everything you have." Illisa then pleaded for mercy and since then he became kind and giving.

21 King Sankhapala

Once, Bodhisattva was born as Prince Duyyodhana of Rajagaha. When he reached his youth, his father became an ascetic and left for the forest crowning him as the king. Now the forest was frequented by a pious naga king named Sankhapala. Impresed with the ascetic's wisdom, Sankhapala visited him regularly to hear his discourses. One day, Duyyodhana came to visit his father and he met the wise Sankhapala in the hermitage. He was fascinated with Sankhapala's ideologies and wished to follow in his footsteps. After many years, when Duyyodhana died, he was reborn in the naga kingdom under the name Sankhapala and became an ascetic. One day, while he was in the middle of his meditation, some men attacked him. They pierced his body and fastened him with ropes to torture him. But the king did not show them any sign of anger. A pious man named Alara saw the ascetic and rescued him from the hands of those cruel man.

22 Prince Duttakumara

One day, while bathing in the river, Prince Duttakumara of Benaras was swept away by the wild current. Bodhisattva, who was that time an ascetic, rescued him along with a drowning rat, a parrot and a snake. In gratitude, the rat, the snake and the parrot promised to share their wealth with him whenever the ascetic would require it. Duttakuma too promised he would provide Bodhisattva with four requisites when the time comes. A few years later, when Duttakumara had become the king of Benaras, Bodhisattva visited his kingdom. But Duttakumara refused to help him in any way and ordered his men to hang him publicly. "It's true that a log pays better respect than men!" Bodhisattva cried aloud. When the people knew the truth, they killed the cruel king and the Bodhisattva was coronated their new king.

23 The Lion in Bad Company

A young lion once became friends with a sly wolf and took the wolf back to his den. The lion's father, wise with age, did not approve of his friendship with the clever wolf and advised the young lion to be cautious. But the lion paid no attention to his father's warning. One day the wolf wanted to eat a horse and he took the young lion to the riverside where the king's ponies used to come for bathing. He urged the lion to hunt one of them and after the lion killed one pony, they both had a sumptuous meal. When the father lion came to know about this, he scolded his son for killing the royal pony and warned him not to do so. But at the wolf's provocation, the lion killed one pony after another. Realising that someone was killing his favourite ponies, the king positioned his archers near the river to protect the ponies. Next day when the lion attacked the ponies again, the archers took their aim and shot the lion to death.

24 Noble Jambuka

The king of Benaras brought up three little birds—an owl, a mynah and a parrot as his own children. He named them Vessantara, Kundalini and Jambuka. When they came of age, the king summoned them to his court one day and asked them in turns to advise him as to how he should reign over his kingdom. Each of them identified some flaw in the way the king ruled his kingdom and also warned him that his carelessness over the same would make him pay heavily some day. Their wisdom pleased everyone and the king awarded them the positions of general, treasurer and the commander-in-chief respectively. When the king died, his subjects wanted Jambuka to be their next king, as he was the most sagacious and pious of all. But for Jambuka, the power and wealth that came with the crown meant nothing after the death of the king whom he loved the most. So he inscribed the principles of righteousness on a golden plate and flew away into the forest from where he had come.

25 The King Who Regained His Belongings

Once King Brahmadatta of Benaras conquered the kingdom of Kosala and brought all the Kosala treasure to his kingdom. He put them in iron pots and buried it in the royal garden. Meanwhile, Chatta, the son of the Kosala king, escaped from Kosala and became a sage. After wandering in many places, he reached Benaras. The king, pleased with the ascetic's beautiful words of wisdom, asked him to stay in his garden. With the magical powers that Chatta had learned in Takkashila, he found his treasure in the garden and fled away with it. When King Brahmadatta found out that the treasure was stolen, he was very disturbed. Bodhisattva, who was the king's minister at that time told him, "O Majesty! Chatta has taken what is rightfully his. Then why are you disturbed for the loss of wealth which was never yours." These words calmed the king and he forgot about his stolen treasures.

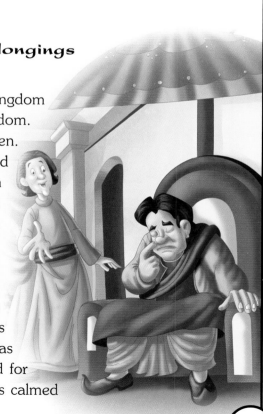

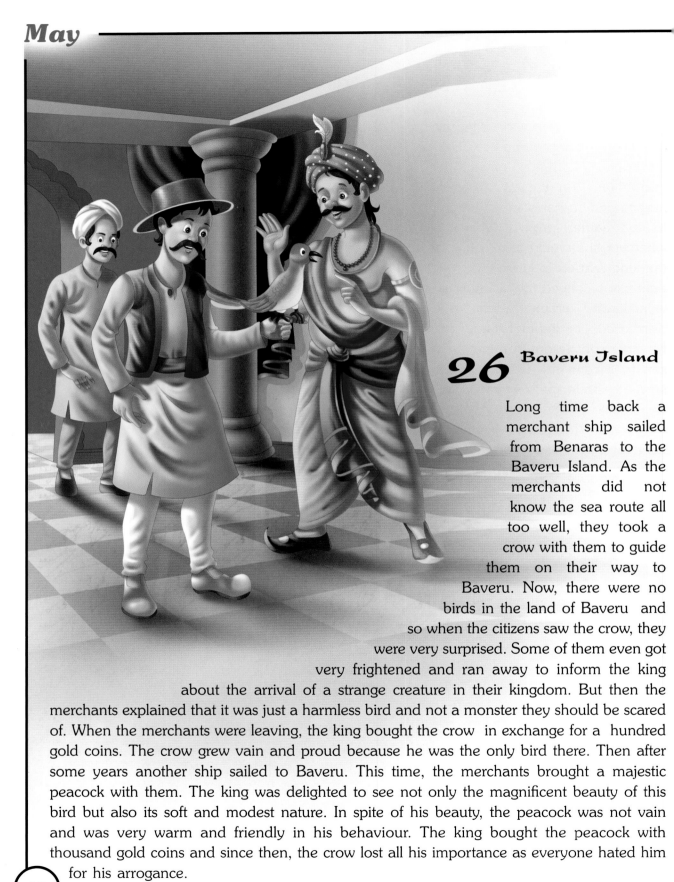

26 Baveru Island

Long time back a merchant ship sailed from Benaras to the Baveru Island. As the merchants did not know the sea route all too well, they took a crow with them to guide them on their way to Baveru. Now, there were no birds in the land of Baveru and so when the citizens saw the crow, they were very surprised. Some of them even got very frightened and ran away to inform the king about the arrival of a strange creature in their kingdom. But then the merchants explained that it was just a harmless bird and not a monster they should be scared of. When the merchants were leaving, the king bought the crow in exchange for a hundred gold coins. The crow grew vain and proud because he was the only bird there. Then after some years another ship sailed to Baveru. This time, the merchants brought a majestic peacock with them. The king was delighted to see not only the magnificent beauty of this bird but also its soft and modest nature. In spite of his beauty, the peacock was not vain and was very warm and friendly in his behaviour. The king bought the peacock with thousand gold coins and since then, the crow lost all his importance as everyone hated him for his arrogance.

27   The Three Princes Leave the Palace

Once upon a time, a king had three beautiful sons. The first two sons were born of the chief queen and the third one was born to the younger queen. When the princes grew up, the younger queen requested the king to crown her son as the next king according to his earlier promise that he would grant whatever she would ask of him as a boon. But the king refused to grant this wish as the throne rightfully belonged to the eldest son. The queen went away visibly angry and very much displeased. Fearing that she might cause harm to his elder sons in order to make it possible for her son to ascend the throne, he ordered his elder sons to leave the kingdom and live in the forest until his death. Reluctantly, the two princes set out for the jungle. The youngest prince who was very fond of his two elder brothers also joined them in their journey.

28   The Water-Sprite Captures the Two Princes

The three princes walked for miles and reached the jungle. They were very tired and the eldest prince asked his youngest brother to fetch some water from the river for all of them to drink. Now, in this river there lived a water-sprite who had the power to cast a spell on anyone who could not give the right answer to her question, "What are good fairies like?" When the youngest prince went to the river, the nymph asked him her question. The prince answered, "Like the stars and the moon." The answer was incorrect and the nymph took him in her power and carried him away with her into her cave. As time passed and the prince did not return, the elder prince got worried about his younger brother's well-being. He said to the other prince, "Dear brother, will you please go to the river and see why he is taking so long." The second prince walked down to the river. He too was asked the same question by the nymph and met with the same fate as his brother.

29 The Eldest Prince Rescues His Brothers

When the second prince reached the river, he met the water-nymph who asked him the same question, "What good fairies are like? "Like the sky above us," replied the prince. The answer didn't please the sprite and she dragged the poor boy into her cave. As time passed and none of the brothers returned, the eldest prince got very anxious about the safety of his brothers and went to look for them. When he reached the edge of the river, the water-sprite appeared and asked him the same question. "The pure spirits never harm souls who are kind and calm," replied he. The answer pleased the sprite and she promised to return him one of his brothers. "Bring me my youngest brother. He is my stepmother's only son. If I ask for my other brother and take him back with me, it'll seem that I have done it to secure the throne for myself." The sprite was very impressed with his thoughtful words and returned both his brothers to him.

30 The Careless Lion

Once upon a time there lived a wealthy man who owned a large herd of cattle. He had appointed a man to take care of them. The herdsman used to take the cattle to the nearby forest to graze. Now, the forest was home to a fierce lion. While grazing, the cattle would sniff his presence in the air and they got very scared and restless. This constant fear of the lurking lion did not allow the cows to graze properly and made them very weak. So, they could give only a little milk. When the owner got to know about the reason behind their illness he suggested a plan to the herdsman as to how he could kill the lion. Accordingly, the herdsman caught a little doe in the forest. The lion was very fond of this little doe. The herdsman smeared the doe's body with poison and then released her. Upon meeting the doe after a long time, the lion was overjoyed and without asking where she had been all these days, started licking her poisoned body in delight. The careless lion died of poisoning almost immediately.

31 The Physician's Revenge

Once, the stable where the king's royal elephants were kept caught fire. The fire badly injured some of the royal elephants. The royal physician was called to treat the elephants' wounds. On his way to the palace, the physician lay down under a tree for a nap. Suddenly, something warm dropped on his face. To his disgust, he realised that a crow, perched on a branch above him, had splattered its droppings on his face. Wiping his face, he cursed the crow and went off to the palace. In order to take revenge on the crows, he prescribed crow's fat as the best medicine to heal the elephants. So the royal guards killed a large number of crows every day. Then one day, a crow flew down to the king when the latter was alone and said, "Your Majesty, I have come to tell you that you are doing great injustice to us by following your physician's advice. He is just taking revenge on us. Let me tell you that crows have no body fat. So how can crow fat be used to treat your injured elephants?" On hearing this, the king felt ashamed of what he had done and immediately stopped further slaughter of crows in his kingdom.

Contents

The Story of the Month: Price of Greed

The Story of the Month

Price of Greed

01 Price of Greed

The king of Benaras had a very clever minister who always gave the king sound advice. He not only helped the king in his official matters but also sorted out the king's personal issues. Pleased with his work, the king decided to reward him and appointed him the headman of a remote border village where his only duty was to collect the taxes from the villagers on the king's behalf. The headman gladly accepted his responsibility and went to the village where he was warmly welcomed by the villagers. As he was a representative of their beloved king, the villagers held their headman in great esteem and accepted him as one of them. They completely trusted his decisions and followed his advice without raising a question. However, the clever headman was a greedy man and wanted to hoard as much wealth as he could. So he befriended a group of bandits and made a wicked plan. "I'll take the villagers to the jungle with some excuse and when they are away, you enter the village and rob. But remember you will have to give me half of the loot," the headman struck a deal with the bandit leader. So a day was decided and the headman led the villagers to the nearby jungle as planned, with an excuse to hunt some deer for the village feast. Without the least idea of any foul play, the villagers gleefully accompanied him and sang merrily on the way:

Here we go hand in hand
Singing gaily in a band
Will hunt and feast on deer meat
And dance to the drum beat

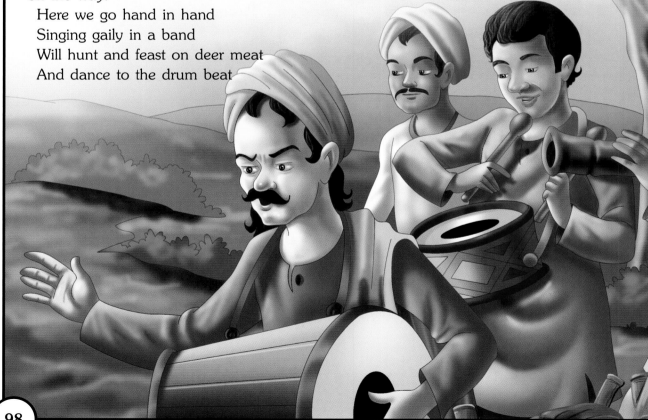

Meanwhile, the robbers entered the village and robbed all the valuables and carried away the cows. On the same day, a merchant from a distant land happened to come to trade in the village. When he saw the empty village, he decided to wait on the outskirts till the villagers returned. The merchant witnessed the robbery. Towards evening, the headman led the villagers back to the village asking them to beat their drums loud so as to chase away the wild animals. But it was just another of his sly plans to caution the bandits of the returning villagers. When they reached the village, the villagers were shocked to see that they had been robbed. "Good Lord! What will we do now? We've been looted," lamented the villagers. Pretending to be very sad and concerned about the villagers, the headman said, "This is indeed a wrong done to us, we have to find the culprit and punish him." Just then the merchant who had witnessed everything walked into the village and said aloud, "This headman of yours is a cheat. He's the one who helped the bandits run away with your valuables by asking you to beat the drums loud while returning from the jungle. He has joined hands with the bandits." The angry villagers reported the matter to the king. On investigation the king found the headman guilty and said, "Your greed has cost you a lot. Now not only will you be given rigorous punishment but your honoured title, respect and luxuries will be taken away." With this, he sentenced the greedy headman to life imprisonment and gave each villager a hundred gold coins and a cow as compensation for their loss.

02 Dhammadhaja, the Righteous

The Bodhisattva was once born as Dhammadhaja, a chaplain in the court of the king of Benaras. Kalaka, the king's captain was a jealous man and he plotted to mar Dhammadhaja's reputation. So he persuaded the king to believe that Dhammadhaja had become more popular than the king. The king became jealous and gave Dhammadhaja a number of difficult tasks to perform. Dhammadhaja did them easily with God's help. Finally, the king asked Dhammadhaja to appoint a park keeper with four virtues. Dhammadhaja again could carry out this task with God's help and found Chattapani, the king's barber who led a pious life free from desires, envy, wine and anger. The king ultimately discovered Kalaka's perfidy and punished him.

03 Two Ways of Beating a Drum

A drummer and his son were once returning through a forest having earned a generous sum of money. Quite happy with their success, the father and son decided to return back to their village. On the way they had to pass through a forest inhabited by robbers who looted travellers. "I must protect myself and father from these robbers," thought the son and started beating his drum loudly. The drummer saw his son and said, "Son, this is not the way to beat the drums. The landlords and their guards play their drums after intervals in a dignified way. We need to do the same to fool the robbers." But the son thought he knew best and continued to beat the drum loud. The robbers heard the drum beats and at once realised that it was not a rich man with tight security. So they attacked the drummer and his son and took away all their hard earned money after having beaten them up.

04 The Story of Romaka Pigeon

The Bodhisattva was once born as Romaka, a pigeon leader and lived on a tree near a hermit's hut. Romaka liked listening to the hermit's sermons and often visited him. But one day the holy hermit went on a pilgrimage and a spurious ascetic came to live in his hut. This hermit was fond of pigeon meat and decided to cook the pigeons for his meal. When Romaka and his friends were approaching the hut as usual, Romaka smelt the odour of the spices and became alert. "Don't fly too near, there's danger," Romaka alerted his followers and they flew away. Seeing the pigeons fly away, the hermit became angry and threw his staff at Romaka. He missed his shot and said, "Sly pigeon, I missed you." At this Romaka replied shrewdly, "You've missed me but won't miss the fire of hell for your wicked nature. I'll reveal your truth to all." Frightened of being caught, the spurious ascetic left the hut for good.

05 The Magic of Patience

The Bodhisattva was a buffalo in one of his rebirths and lived with a mischievous monkey in the forest. Everyday the monkey used to trouble the buffalo either by pulling the buffalo's tail, throwing nuts on the buffalo's head or jumping from the tree top on to the buffalo's back. Though disturbed by the monkey's pranks, the buffalo bore everything patiently without complaining. The other animals of the forest saw this and wondered why the buffalo tolerated all the mischief without losing patience or scolding the monkey. Unable to hold back his curiosity, the elephant one day asked the buffalo why he never punished the monkey. At this the buffalo smiled and said that he was thankful to the monkey for teaching him how to be patient. The monkey who was sitting on the tree top heard this and was ashamed of himself. He came down at once to seek the buffalo's forgiveness and thereafter they became good friends.

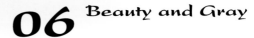

06 Beauty and Gray

The deer leader had two sons—one with a beautiful reddish fur, named Beauty and the other with grey fur, named Gray. One day, the ageing leader called his sons and offered each the leadership of five hundred deer. As harvest time happened to be dangerous for the deer, Beauty and Gray had to lead their herds to the nearby mountain safely till the harvest season was over. "Be careful not to be seen by the villagers, else you'll get killed," advised their father. Gray made his group walk continuously day and night. The villagers killed most of them and he reached the mountains with only a few left. Meanwhile, wise Beauty followed his father's advice and led his herd only in the darkness of the night. He reached the mountain without a single member being hurt. While returning, Gray again led his remaining group in a hurry and all his members got killed, except him. But Beauty returned safely with his entire group. His father was pleased to see this and made Beauty the leader of the deer herd.

07 The Wicked Lady and the Wise Man

A rich merchant had a beautiful, but cruel daughter. One day when the lady was bathing in the river, there was a terrible storm and the lady was swept away by the river current. A holy man who was meditating on the river bank noticed the drowning girl and rescued her. Later he married her. But soon she was tired of living in the forest and persuaded her husband to settle in a village as a butter milkman. One day, the village was attacked by some bandits. Impressed with her beauty the bandit leader made her his wife. She enjoyed the luxurious life of a bandit queen. Fearing that the milkman would come, she wrote a letter to him asking him to come and rescue her from the bandit leader. Believing her, the milkman came looking for her in the bandits' hideout where he was mercilessly beaten up by the bandits. The milkman then revealed how he was deceived by his wife and the bandit leader slayed the wicked lady.

08 A Small Portion of Gruel

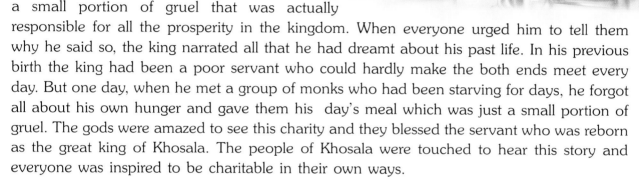

The Bodhisattva, in one of his births, was born as the king of Koshala. He was a benevolent king and his reign was marked by peace and prosperity. One night he dreamt of his previous life and was deeply moved by it. On the following day, the king told his court that it was only a small portion of gruel that was actually responsible for all the prosperity in the kingdom. When everyone urged him to tell them why he said so, the king narrated all that he had dreamt about his past life. In his previous birth the king had been a poor servant who could hardly make the both ends meet every day. But one day, when he met a group of monks who had been starving for days, he forgot all about his own hunger and gave them his day's meal which was just a small portion of gruel. The gods were amazed to see this charity and they blessed the servant who was reborn as the great king of Khosala. The people of Khosala were touched to hear this story and everyone was inspired to be charitable in their own ways.

09 Kesava, the Great

Kesava, was the son of a rich nobleman. But he gave up all his worldly pleasures and became an ascetic. He lived in a hut in the forest and had a number of followers. Kesava had a kind heart and always helped the needy. He would often risk his life to save others in trouble. Kesava attained divine power through his meditation and always used it for the welfare of others. One day a severe drought hit the nearby village and a famine broke out. People were dying out of hunger and thirst. Kesava meditated for seven days continuously and conjured up a river. "O Holy master, you've saved us," the villagers thanked Kesava. More and more people became his disciple. Kesava always taught them that one must never be selfish and be ready to help others, for one is always rewarded for his good actions. Many people thought it to be mere foolishness to risk one's life for others. One day, Kesava was taken seriously ill and seeing him suffer, God himself came down to cure Kesava disguised as a village apothecary.

10 The Doe Who Saved Her Husband's Life

Once there lived a stag who had a beautiful and devoted wife. One day while going to drink water in a pond with his friends, the stag got trapped in a hunter's net. "Help…I'm trapped," shouted the helpless deer. The doe heard her husband's cries and came looking for him. Seeing him in danger, his friends deserted him. Meanwhile, the doe came and saw her husband's pitiable plight. "My dear, how do I get you out of this trap," cried the doe, refusing to leave her husband all alone. She stood by the trap and waited for the hunter along with her husband. When at last the hunter came, the doe fell at his feet and pleaded for her husband's life to be spared in return for hers, "Please do make a bed of grass and kill me first. Then you can enjoy the feast." The hunter was amazed to see such great love and spared the stag's life.

11 The Begging Monks

A group of hermits who went around seeking alms were once subjected to greed and thought, "Why do we need to work hard at all? We can just go around and ask for whatever we need from the villagers. That way we would lead a comfortable life." So the hermits started demanding rather than humbly taking what they were offered. Annoyed, the villagers started avoiding the hermits. A few months later, their guru Kassappa visited them and the villagers avoided him too, thinking he would be as greedy as his disciples. Kassappa was shocked at the villagers' behaviour. When he came to know the cause of this behaviour, he went to Buddha and sought his advice. Buddha summoned the greedy hermits and rebuked them saying, "Beggars can't be choosers. You are supposed to seek alms and not beg to hoard wealth." The hermits realised their mistake and sought his forgiveness.

12 The Parrot on the Fig Tree

The Bodhisattva was born as a parrot in one of his births and lived in a fig tree. He enjoyed eating the ripe fruits of the tree and lived happily. After a few years, the fig tree became old and stopped bearing any fruit. Yet the parrot refused to leave the tree and go elsewhere like the other parrots had done.

Sakka, the king of gods, disguised himself as a goose and asked the parrot why he had not deserted the tree yet. "I cannot forsake my friend who has fed me for years," replied the parrot. Sakka was pleased to hear this and returning to his own form said, "I'm impressed with your feelings for the tree. Ask me what you want." The parrot then bowed his head in respect and said, "Lord, my friend has given me shelter for years. Bless him with the ability to bear fruits all throughout the year like before." "So be it," said Sakka and once again the fig tree became lively and replete with fruits.

13 The Woodpecker and the Ungrateful Tiger

A lion was once writhing in pain as a bone had got stuck in his throat. "Please help me…" cried the lion. A woodpecker who was sitting on a nearby tree heard the tiger and came forward to help him. The woodpecker pulled out the bone from the tiger's throat with his long beak. A couple of days later, driven by hunger, the woodpecker went around looking for food. He had been starving for sometime. Suddenly, he saw the tiger whom he had saved. The tiger was eating a deer. Sure that the tiger would definitely offer to share his food when he saw him, the woodpecker went up to the tiger and greeted him, "Hello friend, how are you?" The selfish tiger looked at the woodpecker and roared angrily and chased the woodpecker away. The God of the forest was angry at the tiger's mean behaviour and volunteered to punish the ungrateful tiger by making him blind. But the woodpecker refused to punish the tiger saying that when he had helped the tiger, he had not expected anything in return.

14 The Story of Vinilaka

A golden gander had three sons. One son, born of a crow, was named Vinilaka. The two other sons were born of a beautiful goose. Vinilaka was black and ugly and lived with his mother in Mithila while the other two sons were fair and comely like their father. The two young ganders decided to bring Vinilaka to stay with them and went to Mithila. Vinilaka happily agreed to come with them. So the two brothers asked Vinilaka to perch on a stick which they held in their beaks and carried him to their abode. On the way, Vinilaka saw the king travelling in his golden carriage, which was drawn by two white horses on either side, and said, "Ah! I'm superior to the king as I'm being carried in the air by two white ganders." This made the young ganders angry but they took Vinilaka to their father and told him what Vinilaka had said. The father then refused to let Vinilaka stay with him and asked them to take him back to Mithila. The young ganders then took Vinilaka away and dropped him in a heap of dung.

15 The Fox, the Hen and the Drum

A fat red hen was busy pecking worms from the ground while a hungry fox watched her from behind a tree. There was a drum on the top of the tree. "Aha! Got a good bait for supper," thought the fox. As he was about to pounce on the hen to eat her, he heard a noise which was made by the drum as the branches of the tree touched its surface. "What a loud noise! It must be some bigger fowl than this hen. I better feed on it for supper than this red hen," thought the greedy fox and decided to let the red hen go. Without further thought, the fox ran out of the bushes, making a loud noise. Hearing this, the hen flew away. The fox struggled hard to climb up to the tree top and alas, what he found was only an empty drum. "Gosh! I'll have to stay without supper tonight because of my greed," sighed the fox and climbed down the tree feeling very sad.

16 The Story of the Jar

Once there lived a king called Sarvamitra. He was a friendly person but having fallen into bad company, took to excessive drinking. The Bodhisattva who was born as a monk saw this and decided to rid the good king of his bad habit. Hanging a jar adorned with flowers around his neck the monk went to meet king Sarvamitra who was busy drinking with his friends. "O King, do consume this exquisite liquor called Sura and get knocked off your senses," said the monk holding the jar in his hand. The words of the monk made the king realise what he meant. He stood up at once with folded hands before the Bodhisattva and said, "Holy soul, I've realised the sin I have been committing being taken to drinking and getting intoxicated. Pray forgive me and take me as your disciple." The Bodhisattva blessed the king and accepted him as his disciple.

17 A Bull Called Delightful

A man had a strong and healthy bull called Delightful. He reared the bull with great love. One day, the young bull decided to do something for his kind master and asked him to declare that his bull was the strongest in town and could pull a hundred loaded carts at one go. The master did as he was advised by Delightful and challenged a rich merchant for a thousand gold coins. On the appointed day, a hundred carts loaded with sand were placed before Delightful. "You dummy bull, drag the carts fast," shouted his master and lashed his whip in the air. Feeling insulted, Delightful did not move an inch forward. His master lost the bet. Delightful then revealed why he had acted so and asked him to challenge the merchant again for two thousand gold coins. This time his master spoke to him sweetly and Delightful dragged the hundred carts in no time and helped his master win the two thousand gold coins.

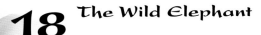

18 The Wild Elephant

The Bodhisattva was once leading his life as an ascetic. He was superior to all the ascetics in their order and everyone used to follow him. There was another ascetic in the same order who was jealous of the Bodhisattva. So, to remove the Bodhisattva from his path, he asked some elephant keepers to intoxicate a ferocious elephant by giving it liquor and then let it loose in the Bodhisattva's path. The ferocious and drunk elephant was let loose on the street and people ran in every direction to save their lives. The Bodhisattva continued walking down the path and looked calm. Suddenly, a frightened woman, who was very flurried, accidentally dropped her child at the feet of the Bodhisattva. The wild elephant walked up to them and as it was about to trample them, the Bodhisattva placed his hand on its forehead and gently stroked it. Suddenly, the wild elephant became calm and bowed in front of him. Everyone was amazed to see this miracle.

19 The Goat Who Saved the Priest

A priest once decided to sacrifice a goat on the altar for the good of his fellow men and himself. While the goat was being prepared for the sacrifice, he remembered his previous births and the unpleasant acts he had committed. Thinking this sacrifice would redeem him from his sins, he laughed out loud. But the very next moment, he cried aloud realising that the priest would be doomed for his act of sacrificing animals, just like he had been for his unwholesome acts in his previous life. Seeing this strange behaviour, the priest enquired about it from the goat. "Learned man, I too was a priest in my previous birth but was doomed to be slaughtered in my five hundred rebirths for my unpleasant acts." Hearing the goat's words, the priest decided to please God with his penance and let the goat free.

20 The Noble Tortoise

Some merchants were sailing in a ship across the seas. Suddenly, a terrible storm hit and their ship was wrecked. The merchants fell into the turbulent water and were struggling for their lives. The Bodhisattva, who was born as a tortoise saw them and was moved with compassion. "I must save them," thought the tortoise and swam towards them. "Do climb on to my back and I'll take you to the shore," offered the tortoise. "Thank you, kind tortoise," said the merchants and climbed on to the tortoise's back. The tortoise swam across the sea and at last they reached the shore. Tired after such a hard swim, the tortoise fell asleep. When he awoke, the tortoise heard the merchants discussing about how hungry they were. Hearing them, the tortoise was moved with pity and decided to offer himself as food to the hungry merchants. "Do feed on my flesh and satisfy your hunger," offered the tortoise and laid flat before them. But the merchants refused to kill their saviour and left.

21 The Pious Son-in-Law

A farmer had a very pious son-in-law, who was a strong believer of the teachings of Lord Buddha. One day, while the farmer was walking through his fields with his son-in-law, he pointed at the crops and said, "Look! This season I'll get a good harvest and become rich." At this, the son-in-law asked the farmer not to be too sure of his success since nothing is certain in this world. Annoyed at his son-in-law's words, the farmer harvested the crops and invited his son-in-law for lunch. Taking the bowl of rice the son-in-law again repeated his warning. Crazy with anger, the farmer snatched the bowl from his son-in-law's hands and the rice fell on to the floor. Pointing at the rice grains on the floor, the son-in-law said, "See, nothing is certain because inspite of having the bowl of rice in my hands, I could not eat it. Everything happens at God's will." The farmer then realised the depth in his son-in-law's words and kept quiet.

22 Sloth

The Bodhisattva was once the minister of the king of Benaras. The king was a very lazy man and spent most of his time idling. He did not take much interest in the matters of the state and this resulted in unrest among the people. His ministers tried to make the king realise his duties but the king refused to listen to anyone saying, "I'm the king and I know what's best." Frustrated, the ministers asked the Bodhisattva to speak to the king. The Bodhisattva knew that the king would not listen to him if he would go and advise the king to be active in carrying out his duties. So he very cleverly narrated the king the story of a lazy tortoise leader who kept sleeping the whole day and did not take care of his group till one day, his group members beat him up and chased him away, choosing an energetic leader to lead them. The king at once realised his vice and from the very next day, changed his ways and became an ideal ruler.

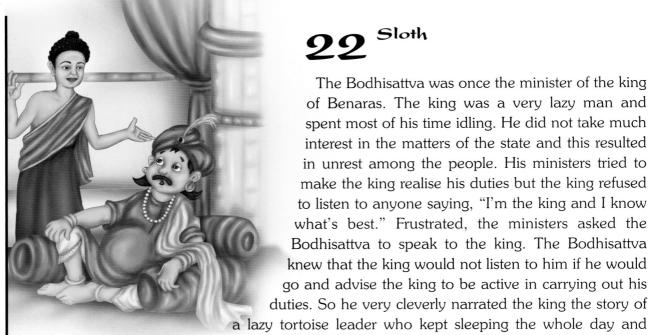

23 The King's Nightmare

Brahmadatta, the king of Benaras, dreamt a horrible dream one night. Fearing that his dream was an indication of some danger, the king called the royal priest and asked him to interpret his dream. "Hmmm…it's a sure sign of some great calamity, My Lord. It might be a threat for your life, for your kingdom or for the royal wealth." Hearing the priest, the king was very worried and requested him to suggest a way of avoiding the disaster. The greedy royal priest saw this to be a golden opportunity to become rich. "My Lord, you'll have to offer the greatest animal sacrifice and must kill, as sacrificial offerings, four of every type of animal that lives." Though sad, the compassionate king gave his consent. The royal priest started the ceremony calling it Four from All sacrifice. But the Bodhisattva, who was also a guest in the ceremony made the king realise that no misfortune can be avoided by taking somebody else's life. The king then at once called off the sacrificial ceremony.

24 The Virtuous Wife

A rich young man and his virtuous wife, Sujata, were travelling through the city in their cart, the husband driving the cart and the beautiful wife walking behind. The king was also passing by at the same time and saw Sujata. Attracted by her beauty, the king decided to have her as his wife. To get rid of her husband, the king

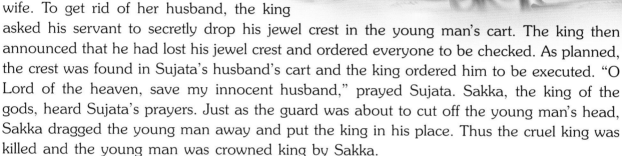

asked his servant to secretly drop his jewel crest in the young man's cart. The king then announced that he had lost his jewel crest and ordered everyone to be checked. As planned, the crest was found in Sujata's husband's cart and the king ordered him to be executed. "O Lord of the heaven, save my innocent husband," prayed Sujata. Sakka, the king of the gods, heard Sujata's prayers. Just as the guard was about to cut off the young man's head, Sakka dragged the young man away and put the king in his place. Thus the cruel king was killed and the young man was crowned king by Sakka.

25 Temptation

A young merchant accompanied by four servants, once set out on a journey to a neighbouring city to seek his fortune. On the way they had to cross a forest inhabited by female demons who attracted travellers by taking the form of beautiful maidens and building mansions on the way. Whosoever got attracted to the demons and went into their mansion, the hungry demons ate them. The merchant had heard about the demons and warned his servants not to get tempted by them. As they approached the deadly forest, the demons appeared in the form of young, attractive maidens looking out of the windows of a huge, beautiful mansion. One of his servants failed to resist the beautiful maidens and went into the mansion on the pretext of taking a rest. The other three servants continued on their journey with their master for a while, but at last they too gave in to their temptations and became easy prey for the hungry demons.

26 Two Ascetics

The Bodhisattva was once born as the king of Gandhara. One day, he saw the lunar eclipse and realised the futility of his kingly life. So he became an ascetic and went to live in the forest. The king of Videha, who was his friend, followed him. The two ascetics stayed together in the forest and went to the village to seek alms daily. One day, one of the ascetics hid some salt for use on the rainy days without his friend's knowledge. When the other ascetic found the salt, he was very displeased with his friend for being selfish and greedy. The ascetic realised his mistake and sought his friend's forgiveness saying, "I'm indeed guilty of being attached to worldly things, my friend. Please forgive me for being selfish." So the two again became friends and led a life of penance.

27 The Mango Thief

A dishonest ascetic lived in a mango grove by the river and did nothing, except guarding and eating the mangoes. He had become an ascetic only to get gifts and donations.

Sakka, the king of gods, saw the wicked ways of the ascetic and deciding to teach him a lesson, plucked all the mangoes, leaving nothing behind. When the ascetic returned, he was very angry and looked around for the thief. He accused four daughters of a merchant who were passing by of stealing the mangoes and searched their bags. But he failed to find any evidence related to the mangoes and allowed them to go. The poor maidens felt insulted and left the garden weeping. Sakka saw this and having lost his temper, appeared before the ascetic in a terrible form. The horrifying sight of Sakka frightened the ascetic and he left the orchard for good.

28 Dhumakari, the Herdsman

There once lived a goatherd called Dhumakari. One day, while Dhumakari's goats were grazing, a herd of mountain deer came to the field. Their beauty attracted Dhumari and he kept looking at them all day long, neglecting his goats. Days passed and Dhumakari completely forgot his goats. Out of hunger, the poor goats became frail and weak. Slowly summer passed and with the advent of autumn, the mountain deer left the plains. Dhumakari went back to the mountains. Being alone, Dhumakari remembered his goats but alas, all his goats had died of starvation.

29 Roaring Bulls with No Fight

King Brahmadatta one night dreamed a strange dream in which he saw four huge bulls come charging from four directions at each other but they returned without fighting. The royal priest advised him to sacrifice animals to avoid any mishap. But the Bodhisattva, who was an ascetic, interpreted the King's dream as an indication of some misfortunes that would befall mankind in the distant future. He said that there would be drought and startvation as dark clouds woud appear but would bring no rain just as the bulls went away without fighting. The King realised that there was no imminent danger and banned the sacrifice of animals.

30 The King and the Hermit

Once a proud, selfish king ruled the kingdom of Benaras. Everday, the king sacrificed an animal to earn penance. One day, a hermit came begging at the palace. The cruel king chased him away saying he had nothing to spare for people who just came begging. At this, the hermit said, "My Lord, you're killing animals every day to earn penance. But charity is the greatest penance on earth. When you can't give life, you have no right to take away life," and left. The proud king realised the truth of life and became the hermit's disciple, giving away all luxuries of life

Contents

The Story of the Month: The Story of Ruru Deer

The Story of the Month

The Story of Ruru Deer

01 The Story of Ruru Deer

Long ago, the Bodhisattva was born as a golden deer named Ruru. No other deer was as lovely as him. His golden body shone like the sun; his lotus eyes sparkled like the stars. He lived in the dense jungles in close friendship with other animals. The tiger, the lion, the snake, the monkeys, the elephants and all the birds loved Ruru dearly, for he was very kind-hearted and gentle. In sickness and in health, Ruru was always there to help them. If ever there was a fight, Ruru mediated and solved the problem. If someone fell ill, Ruru rushed to his side. One day, while roaming the forest, Ruru heard a heart-wrenching cry. He turned around and saw a man drowning in the river nearby. Without wasting a second, Ruru dived into the river. He grabbed the man with his front legs and pulled him with all his might towards the bank. Emerging from the cold water, the shivering man folded his hands and said, "Thank you gentle creature. You have shown unmatchable courage, kindness and strength! I am indebted to you forever!" "Sir, do not say such things for it is difficult to believe what men promise!" replied gentle Ruru and walked away. The man returned safe and happy to his village where he spoke about his encounter with the golden deer Ruru. When the news reached the king, he decided to hunt down the precious animal and keep it as a trophy in his palace. The man was summoned to the palace. "If you help me catch the golden deer I shall reward you handsomely!" the king said. Overwhelmed with greed, the man immediately promised to take the king to Ruru. They reached the forest with a group of soldiers and were surprised to see Ruru standing there as if waiting for them.

"Welcome to my humble abode, sir," said Ruru warmly to the king. Both the man and the king were shocked. "How did Ruru know that we were coming to the forest?" the king asked the man. In a haste to get hold of his desired object, the king aimed his arrow at Ruru. But lo and behold, Ruru transformed into a handsome man right before their eyes! He had a bright halo behind his head and his eyes shone like stars. "Who ... who are you?" the king asked nervously. "I am the Almighty and I know everything that men think or do!" declared the man. He then turned to the man he had once rescued and said, "Remember, I had said that I don't believe the promises men make, for more often than not, they turn out to be deceitful as yourself!" "I do, I do!" stammered the man, who was almost on the verge of tears. "Please forgive me, O Lord!" he begged. "I was blinded by greed and had lost my good sense!" "Forgive me too," cried the king.

The next instant the Almighty once again became the golden deer Ruru. He blessed the two men and slowly went away. The king and the man returned with the precious realisation that one should stay away from greed as it always leads one astray.

02 Kshantivadin

Once there was an ascetic named Kshantivadin. A few young queens of a nearby kingdom came to listen to him and were so charmed by his saintly look that they forgot all about their king who had followed them with his servants. Seeing his queens sitting absorbed in front of Kshantivadin, he misunderstood their purpose. In a fit of rage and jealousy, he chopped off the ascetic's arms, legs, ears and nose and left him writhing in pain. Having satisfied himself the king was about to leave the spot when all of a sudden the earth opened up as if to swallow him. Seeing this, the king's servants got scared and thought that Kshantivadin had cursed the king for his cruelty. They begged him for mercy and asked him to spare the king. Kshantivadin told them that he never wanted to hurt the king but believed that the king's jealous nature needed to change, as it would bring nothing but misery for one and all. Saying this, Kshantivadin died, and, soon after, the king's reign also came to an end and his kingdom got destroyed.

03 The Price of Sin

Bodhisattva was once born as Jotipala, the great archer. Later he became an ascetic and came to be known as Sarabhanga. Sarabhanga had many disciples and sent them to various places to preach the importance of leading a virtuous life. But unfortunately, they were often ill-treated. Once Kisavaccha, his chief follower was abused by King Dandaki of Kumbhavati. Kisavaccha was heartbroken and went back to his home near the Godavari where he breathed his last. Such was his piety that during his funeral, the gods showered beautiful flowers on his pyre as a mark of respect. The kingdom of Kumbhavati together with King Dandaki soon perished as punishment for ill-treating Kisavaccha and abetting his death. When the kings of neighbouring states came to know about this, they felt scared. Many of them atoned for their past sins and started living a virtuous life.

04 The Cunning Wolf

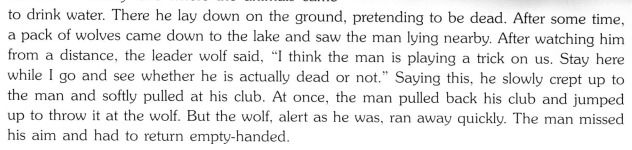

One day, a few townsmen went to a jungle for a picnic carrying baskets full of delicious food. Having travelled far, they felt so hungry that they ate up everything leaving not a morsel for dinner. "Make the fire ready. I will get some fresh meat for all of us," volunteered one of them. So saying, he took a club and went to a nearby lake where the animals came to drink water. There he lay down on the ground, pretending to be dead. After some time, a pack of wolves came down to the lake and saw the man lying nearby. After watching him from a distance, the leader wolf said, "I think the man is playing a trick on us. Stay here while I go and see whether he is actually dead or not." Saying this, he slowly crept up to the man and softly pulled at his club. At once, the man pulled back his club and jumped up to throw it at the wolf. But the wolf, alert as he was, ran away quickly. The man missed his aim and had to return empty-handed.

05 The Treasure in the Well

Once upon a time, the Bodhisattva was born as a merchant. One day, he was travelling with a large caravan to a faraway land. One the way, while passing through a wood, they came across a well. It was dry and appeared unused for years. By then, the travellers were very thirsty and decided to dig the well for water. They dug and dug and lo, there was a big chest lying under the ground. They opened the chest and were stunned to see it full of sparkling gold coins. Their eyes glistened with greed and they decided to dig the well deeper hoping that some more treasures could be lying underneath. Only the Bodhisattva did not approve of the idea. "My friends, it's not wise to dig more. Let's be happy with what we have got. Too much greed can bring trouble," said he. But his friends laughed him off and went on with the digging. A naga king who lived under the ground was enraged at this disturbance, and, together with his band of poisonous snakes, killed everyone sparing only the Bodhisattva.

06 Two Dining Rooms

Once, Buddha appeared in the dream of a little boy and took him along to show Heaven and Hell. They entered a hall with a big dining table with delicious dishes spread all over it. Then suddenly some sad-faced ghosts appeared and jostled with each other to eat their favourite dishes. But they fumbled the food with very long chopsticks and could not eat even a morsel. At last, they started fighting among themselves. Then the boy was taken to another hall. This dining hall was similar to the previous one, the only difference being that here some cheerful people were gathered at the table. The boy was just wondering how they would manage to eat with the long chopsticks, when he was surprised to see that each of them started feeding the person sitting next to him. They fed each other by turns and everyone tasted enough of every delightful dish. Buddha then turned to the boy and said, "Did you note how everything in life depends on the way you are and the way you behave? You yourself can make a certain place Heaven or Hell by your own actions."

07 The Snake and the Green Frog

The Bodhisattva was once born as a green frog. One day some fishermen came to the lake where he lived and set a wicker cage under the water to catch fish. A water snake, who was very hungry and was looking for fish to eat, came to the spot and fell inside the cage. The fish saw the snake and attacked him. Badly bitten all over, he somehow managed to escape and came to the edge of the river. Just then, the green frog came hopping by to save the fish. Seeing the frog the snake called out, "O wise frog, the fish you're trying to save have just now attacked and tried to kill me. Tell me, were they right in doing so?" The frog looked at the snake and said, "Of course, they were. When a fish enters your territory don't you kill and eat it? So also the fish have attacked you when you came their way."

08   The Lean Cat and the Fat cat

A poor woman had a cat who was very lean as the woman could not give her enough to eat. One day the cat was sitting on the verandah, when she saw another cat passing by. Seeing the latter so healthy and fine the lean one enquired what the fat cat fed on. "Oh, at the palace, of course! When the royal feast is spread on the table, I steal away a good amount of roasted meat or fried trout," replied the fat cat. At the mention of these mouth-watering dishes the lean cat made up her mind to visit the palace the following day. When her mistress came to know about her plans, she warned her of all the possible dangers. But the cat paid no heed and went to the palace the next morning. As soon as she entered the dining hall, the aroma of fried fish filled her nose and

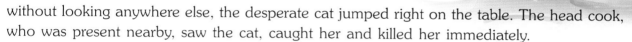

without looking anywhere else, the desperate cat jumped right on the table. The head cook, who was present nearby, saw the cat, caught her and killed her immediately.

09   The Faithful Dog

Once the Bodhisattva was born as a very good-looking dog whom everyone in the neighbourhood loved. He was very loyal to his master and his family. However, the master noticed that every night he went missing and came back in the morning completely soaked in water. Finally the master discovered that the dog swam to the other side of the river every night to keep watch on another family. He was furious and scolded the dog hard. That night, the dog appeared to him in his dream and told him that he goes to guard the other house as a way of paying a debt incurred in his past life. He owed the owner of that house some money and when he covered his remaining debt, he would stop going there. The next morning, the master tied some money around the dog's neck and in the night, when the dog went to the house across the river, he took off the money, threw it inside through the window, and came back happy that he would never have to go back again as he had paid back his loan.

10 The Beautiful Fish

Once upon a time there were two beautiful fish. One belonged to the River Ganga and the other lived in the River Yamuna. One day, when the waters were in high tide, the two fish met each other at the confluence of the two rivers. One fish said to the other, "Yesterday I saw myself in the mirror which I found under the water. I was amazed to see my beauty. I guess I am the most beautiful fish in the whole world." At this, the other fish burst into laughter. "O what a vain fish you are! How could you think you are the most beautiful fish on earth? Why, everyone says that I am the prettiest one," bragged the other fish and they broke into a terrible fight. Just then, they caught sight of a tortoise coming their way. The two fish decided to take his opinion on the issue and called out to him, "Hello, sir, can you say who among the two of us is the most beautiful?" The tortoise looked at both of them and said, "Oh, I find both of you beautiful. But I am sure I am more beautiful than either of you."

11 The Foolish Monkeys

One day the gardener of the royal garden decided to visit his friend in a nearby town. So, he went to a pack of monkeys that lived in the garden and said, "Could you do me a favour by watering the young plants tomorrow? I shall be away at my friend's, and there will be no one to water them." The leader of the monkeys readily agreed to help . So the gardener told him, "Please see that the plants get enough water—not too much, not too little." The next day the monkeys took the watering pots and went to water the plants. "Make sure that the plants get enough water," commanded the leader. "But sir, how shall we know that a particular plant has had enough water or not?" asked a young monkey. The leader monkey had no good answer . So he thought for a while and said, " Just pull up each young plant and see the length of the roots. Give a great deal of water to those which have long roots and give only a little to those with short ones." The next morning when the gardener came back, he found all the young plants dead.

12 The Beautiful Unmadayanti

Once upon a time, there lived a pious and benevolent king. A rich merchant in his kingdom had a lovely daughter named Unmadayanti. Her father wanted to marry her off to the king. When the king received the proposal from the man, he sent his royal priest to find out whether the girl was suitable enough to become the queen of the land. When the Brahmin reached her house, the girl attended him with great modesty and courtesy. But the Brahmin, even against his own principles, felt infatuated with her. He came to the conclusion that the girl would all the more distract the king and he would forget his responsibilities towards his kingdom. He went to the king and told him that the girl was 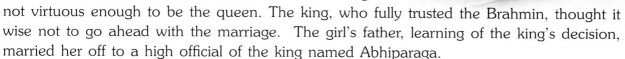 not virtuous enough to be the queen. The king, who fully trusted the Brahmin, thought it wise not to go ahead with the marriage. The girl's father, learning of the king's decision, married her off to a high official of the king named Abhiparaga.

13 The King and Unmadayanti

A few days after Unmadayanti got married to Abhiparaga it was time for the Kaumudi festival. The king decided to take a round of his kingdom to see the celebration that was going on. As he was riding through the town, he came across the house of Abhiparaga and saw Unmadayanti standing by the window of her house. He immediately fell in love with her. But wise as he was, he knew that it would not be proper to show his weakness and tried hard to control himself. Abhiparaga, however, sensed that the king was not his usual self and met him secretly in his chamber. The king confessed his love to him. Abhiparaga skillfully engaged him in a discussion about right and wrong, the importance of virtue and a king's code of conduct. Listening to Abhiparaga, the king came back to his senses and realised his mistake. He decided to forget Unmadayanti and ruled efficiently ever after.

14 The Wicked Monarch

Once there lived in Kampilla a king named Pancala, who was notorious for his wicked ways. He never cared about his subjects and took great pleasure in oppressing them. The Bodhisattva was at that time a tree spirit residing high up in the Gandatindu tree and could see everything that was happening in the kingdom. One night, the Bodhisattva appeared in the bedchamber of the king and said to him, "O king, all your life you have amassed wealth but could never get anybody's respect or love. People obey you out of fear and not out of love or respect. Tomorrow take a round of your kingdom and find out for yourself what everyone thinks of you." Saying this, the Bodhisattva disappeared. The next day, the king decided to travel across his kingdom in disguise. Everywhere he went, he found men, women and even little children cursing him. He realised that he had failed as a king. Since then, he spent his life doing good deeds.

15 The Queen of Kushinagar Prays for a Son

Once upon a time, King Okkaka ruled over the kingdom of Mallas. The king had everything and yet was not happy because he was childless. Now, the king had sixty thousand queens among whom Silavati was his favourite. She was very beautiful and pious. Seeing her husband in so much anxiety, the queen decided to try and please the gods. For days and nights she prayed hard without taking food or water. Seeing her devotion, Sakka, the king of gods, took pity and appeared before her. "O virtuous queen! Open your eyes. Your prayers have brought me here. I am very pleased with your devotion. I shall grant you a boon. Ask for whatever you wish to have," said the god. The queen opened her eyes and bowed to him in respect. Then she said, "O Lord! The only thing I want is a son." Sakka smiled and granted her wish.

16 Two Sons Were Born to the Queen of Kushinagar

The king of the gods was pleased with Silavati's devotion and said, "O virtuous queen, I grant you two sons. One will be ugly but a man of great wisdom. The other will be handsome but foolish. Tell me, which one of them you would want to have as your first son." Silavati chose to have the wise one as her first child. Sakka presented her with a bunch of kusa grass, a heavenly robe, sandalwood, a coral flower and a lute. Then he touched her forehead and blessed her. The queen returned to her chamber and informed the king about the happy incident. Days passed and a baby was born to queen Silavati and was named Kusa after the kusa grass. When Prince Kusa was just a toddler, the queen had her second baby who was named Jayampati. From his early childhood, the elder prince showed signs of being capable and virtuous and by the time he was sixteen, he mastered all the liberal arts.

17 The King of Kushinagar Looks for a Bride for His Son

King Okkaka of Kushinagar was aging and wanted to coronate Prince Kusa before leaving the world. But the prince was not yet married as he felt that he was too ugly to be loved by any woman. His mother tried repeatedly to persuade him, and finally, seeing no other way to avoid marriage, he made a plan. He painted an image of a beautiful nymph and set a condition that only if his parents could find him a wife as beautiful as her, he would be ready to marry. His parents sent their emissaries to different lands to find a woman whose beauty matched that of the image. Now, King Sagal of the kingdom of Madda had eight daughters each of whom was known for extraordinary beauty. The eldest among them was Pabhavati who closely resembled the lovely nymph in the image. When the messengers of King Okkaka placed the image near a pond, all were amazed to find that it resembled princess Pabhavati.

18 Prince Kusa of Kushinagar Marries Princess Pabhavati

King Okkaka and King Sagal finalised the marriage of prince Kusa and princess Pabhavati. Meanwhile, Queen Silavati, knowing very well that no beautiful woman would like to have an ugly husband like Kusa, told King Sagal that it was not in their family custom for a bride to see her husband's face before a child was born. Thus Kusa and Pabhavati got married without seeing each other. One day, Kusa expressed to his mother his desire to see his bride in broad daylight. So Silavati took Pabhavati on a visit to the royal shed. When the two ladies were strolling in the shed, looking at the fine animals, King Kusa, dressed as an elephant trainer, stole a glimpse at his bride and her beauty overwhelmed him. In an attempt to draw her attention, he playfully threw elephant's dung at the princess' back and this enraged her. Silavati admonished the trainer mockingly and pacified the queen.

19 King Kusa Reveals His Identity to His Wife

Queen Pabhavati one day expressed her desire to see a glimpse of her husband. So Silavati organised a royal procession in which the king sat behind his handsome brother Jayampati on a majestic elephant. Pabhavati got a glimpse of Jayampati from her palace window and took him for her husband. Suddenly, her eyes caught sight of Kusa who was waving at her playfully. Soon, it occurred to her that something was wrong, as it was not likely for an ordinary person to behave so audaciously with a royal lady. She sent her attendant to investigate the matter. But King Kusa, learning that she had suspected the truth, forbade the maid to divulge anything to her. Now, King Kusa was so infatuated by Pabhavati's beauty that he could hardly control his desire to see her once again. So one day, he hid himself behind a large lotus in the royal pond where Pabhavati had her bath and while Pabhavati was bathing, Kusa appeared before her and revealed his true identity.

20 Queen Pabhavati Unites with King Kusa

Pabhavati was shocked to know that the ugly prince was her real husband. She cried aloud to God, "I was celebrated for my beauty. What harm did I do anyone that I should have such an ugly husband?" But most of all, she felt humiliated by this deception as she felt that she had the right to know the truth before her marriage. Shocked and pained, she left her husband and returned to her father. King Kusa realised that her anger was justified and followed her to Madda to bring her back. He met her and said, "My dear queen, forgive me for this deception. You consider yourself unfortunate to be married to an ugly man like me, but I can assure you that my heart does not resemble my appearance." His words softened Pabhavati's heart. She remembered all that she had heard about the king's wisdom. She realised that it was not proper to judge a person by his appearance and came back to him.

21 Racing with the Sun

Once upon a time, the Bodhisattva was the king of ninety thousand geese. One day, while travelling, the king of Benaras caught sight of him and was charmed by his graceful manners. He became a friend of the king of Benaras and lived in his royal garden. One day, two young geese were fighting with each other as to who was the stronger among them and decided to test each other by trying their speed against that of the sun. When Bodhisattva heard this, he warned them repeatedly of the danger. But they didn't pay any heed and flew upwards. The Bodhisattva, too, flew with them and caught hold of them when they were too exhausted to fly any more. Later on, he raced against the sun and emerged victorious. The king of Benaras, who watched everything from his palace, was amazed at the goose's speed. He congratulated the goose and asked whether there was any other creature swifter than him. The king of geese smiled and said, "O great king! When a man falls from honour, his moral decay is a thousand-fold swifter than my speed."

22 The Wishing Cup

Once, the Bodhisattva was born as a rich merchant. He led an honest life and then passed away leaving behind all his wealth to his lazy son. Because of his good deeds he was reborn in heaven as Sakka. Meanwhile, his son squandered away all his father's money and soon became poor. Sakka watched everything from heaven and felt sad for his son. So one day he appeared to his son in his old self and said, "My Son, I am giving you a second chance to lead a comfortable life." Saying this, he handed him a "wishing cup" and continued, "Take this, Bhadraghata. Whenever you need something badly, hold this cup and ask for it and you'll get whatever you want." Soon, with the help of the cup, the son became rich again. But he didn't mend his ways. One day, in a drunken fit, he threw the cup in the air and it broke into pieces. Soon after he turned poor again.

23 Mahaasona and Suhanu

Once upon a time, there lived a miserly king in Benaras who had an untamed horse named Mahaasona. One day, some horse dealers came to Benaras with some good horses. The king liked the horses but unwilling to spend much, he set his wild horse free among the horses brought by the dealers. The wild horse bit the other horses savagely and the king bought the wounded horse at a lower price. The horse dealers understood the trick and sought a wise minister's help who advised them to come back with a very strong horse. So accordingly, the next time they brought with them a strong horse named Suhanu. This time too, the king played the same trick. But, much to the king's dismay, when Mahaasona and Suhanu met, they didn't fight. Instead, they showed affection for each other. Seeing the king's bewilderment, the minister said, "My lord! Even horses recognise each other's virtues." The felt ashamed and gave the horse dealers their due.

24 The Woman and the Three Bandits

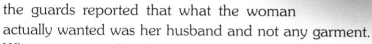

Once the king's guards mistook three farmers for bandits and dragged them to the king. As the king ordered for a trial, a poor woman entered the court lamenting. The king ordered his men to give her a loose-fitting garment thinking that she needed cover from the rough weather. But soon the guards reported that what the woman actually wanted was her husband and not any garment.

When summoned before the king, the woman admitted that the report was true. The woman confessed that one of them was her husband, one was her son and the other was her brother. When the king asked her who among them she wished most to be released the woman replied, "O majesty, if given the choice, I would like to have my brother back because he is irreplaceable. Later on, I can remarry and have another husband and son." This pleased the king and he released all of them.

25 The Preacher and the Student

Once, the Bodhisattva was born as Karandiya, a young Brahmin studying under a renowned teacher in Takkasila. The teacher had a habit of preaching moral laws to anyone and everyone he met, regardless of the fact whether they were willing to listen or not. One day, Karandiya went out with his friends to a nearby village. On the way, while crossing a jungle, he noticed a cave and started throwing stones at it. After they returned, the students informed the teacher about his strange behaviour. The latter asked Karandiya the reason behind his strange action.

Karandiya expressed his surprise and said, "Why can't I try to make the world level when you think you can make the whole world moral?" The teacher realised his mistake and stopped his habit of preaching indiscriminately.

26 The Best Friends

Once a sickly stray pup lived by the shed of a royal bull elephant. Attracted by the sweet smell of rice that was cooked for the elephant, he began sneaking into the shed every day to eat the leftovers. The elephant was compassionate and never said anything to the pup. Days passed and they developed a friendship rarely seen between elephants and pups. The pup gradually grew up to be a handsome dog. One day, a man from a distant village was passing by the elephant shed and his eyes fell on the handsome dog. He liked the dog and took him away to his village. The elephant was heartbroken at this unexpected separation and refused to eat or work properly. Concerned about his elephant's well-being, the king sent his wise minister to see what could be done. Seeing the elephant, the minister realised that he was not sick but was sad from some deep loss. When he learned about the dog, he brought him back to the elephant. The two friends were overjoyed to see each other and soon the elephant recovered his health.

27 Jayddisa, Alinasattu and the Ogre

Once upon a time, there lived in Kampilla a king named Jayaddisa. He had a son named Alinasattu who was known to be very pious and generous. One day, before setting out with his son for hunting, Jayaddisa promised a Brahmin named Nanda that he would give the latter a thousand gold coins after he returned from his expedition. But an ogre residing in the jungle captured the king while the latter was on his way back. The king remembered the promise he had made to the Brahmin and pleaded with the ogre to let him go so he could keep his word. When the ogre refused to listen, Alinasattu intervened and volunteered to take Jayaddisa's place so that Jayaddisa could go to the Brahmin. Impressed by Alinasattu's courage, the ogre released his father. The son and the father then went home safely.

28 The Messenger of Gluttony

Once, the Bodhisattva was born as the king of Benaras who loved good food and loved sharing his food with others. He always ate his meals sitting on a pavilion in full view of his people. One day, a greedy man saw him eating delicious dishes and wished to taste them. So he came up to him and introduced himself as a messenger, as only messengers had free access to the king. Then, without talking any further, he snatched some food from the table and thrust it into his mouth. Seeing this, the king's men came running to catch hold of him but the king forbade them and invited the man to share his food. After he finished his meal, the king asked him about the message he had brought for him. The man replied, "O king, I am the messenger of gluttony!" Pleased with the man's truthfulness, the king rewarded him with a thousand cows.

29 Magha the wise

Once there lived a wise man named Magha. He taught his fellow villagers how to be kind and compassionate and stay away from sins. The village headman was however jealous of Magha and falsely alleged to the king that all his fellow villagers were bandits. The king believed him and ordered them all to be trampled to death by elephants. But seeing their calm and fearless faces, the elephants refused to trample Magha and his fellow villagers. The king was amazed to see this. Then Magha explained, "We don't do any wrong and so live in peace and fearlessness. The elephants saw our inner strength. It made them fearless of their trainers and they refused to trample us." Hearing these wise words, the king realised that these people couldn't be bandits. After learning the truth, he released them and punished the real culprit.

30 The Two Parrots

Once, the Bodhisattva was born as a parrot called Radha. He had a younger brother named Potthapada. They lived in Benaras with a Brahmin who loved them very much and cared for them as his children. One day the Brahmin had to go to a distant village, but before leaving asked the parrots to keep an eye on his wicked wife. After he left, the woman started keeping bad company. The younger parrot got worried at this rebuked the woman for her wicked ways. Enraged at this the woman killed him. When the Brahmin came back, he asked Radha about his wife and about Potthapada's whereabouts. "It is not wise for me to speak of things which are not conducive to my well-being whether they have happened or not, otherwise, I'll face the same fate as Potthapada," replied Radha and flew away.

31 The Two Swans

Once in the beautiful Manas lake of the Himalayas there lived two majestic swans named Dhritarastra and Sumukha. The beauty and the elegance of these two swans were so celebrated across the world that the king of Varanasi became desperate to have them in his garden. So he constructed a beautiful lake which rivalled the splendour of the Manas Lake. Learning about the virgin lake, most of the swans left the Manas Lake and flew down to it to make the lake their new home. Dhritarastra and Samukha, though at first reluctant to change their abode, joined them too. When the king heard about their arrival, he appointed a fowler to catch the two swans. The fowler hid some snares on the spots frequented by the two swans and next morning Dhritarastra was trapped. Samukha, though not yet caught, refused to leave his partner alone. When the fowler saw the loyalty of Samukha, his heart filled with compassion and he released Dhritarastra. The two birds thanked him and accompanied him to the king to explain what had happened and save him from punishment. But the king, too, was moved when he heard their story and gave up his desire to capture the swans.

Contents

The Story of the Month: Bhuuridatta

The Story of the Month

Bhuuridatta

01 Bhuuridatta

Once upon a time Prince Brahmadatta, the son of the king of Benaras, was exiled from the kingdom. He left Benaras and started living on the banks of the river Yamuna as a mendicant. But in his heart he never accepted this new way of life. One day, while bathing in the Yamuna, he saw a beautiful snake maiden. Her beauty was so captivating that the prince fell in love with her at the first sight. They united and had two children named Sagara Brahmadatta and Samuddaja. When the king of Benaras died, Brahmadatta returned to Benaras and ascended the throne. His children accompanied him while his wife returned to

the world of the nagas or snakes. As the children were accustomed to spending their time beside the Yamuna River, Brahmadatta build a big lake for them to play in. One day, while playing, the children saw a tortoise in the water. As they had never seen a tortoise before, the children got scared and ran to their father. The king ordered his sentries to catch the tortoise and throw it into the river. Once in the river, the tortoise got caught in a whirlpool and was dragged to the naga world. King Dhatarattha was not happy to see a strange creature in his kingdom and asked him his purpose of visiting the naga world. Though scared, the tortoise used his presence of mind and said, "O great king! I am the messenger of King Brahmadatta of Benaras. It is the sincere desire of our king to marry his daughter to you. It is with this purpose that I have come." The naga king was overjoyed to get the royal proposal and sent his messengers to the king of Benaras. Meanwhile, the tortoise disappeared from the scene. Now, Brahmadatta was horrified at the idea of marrying off his daughter to the naga king. But he didn't dare to enrage the naga king and thus Samuddaja was married to Dhatarattha. They had five children one of whom was the Bodhisattva who was at that time known as Bhuuridatta. He was a pious soul and never strayed from the path of virtue. He observed fast regularly and prayed to God lying coiled around an anthill. One day, while he was observing fast, a Brahmin named Alambayana and his companion saw him and took him captive. So devoted was he to his principles that Bhuuridatta didn't bite them even to save himself. Alambayana carried him along and in order to make some easy money made the snake dance in front of large groups of spectators. Still Bhuuridatta never retaliated or bit anyone and continued with his fast. Meanwhile, his family was very worried about him and went around looking for him. Having found him, his brothers and sisters rescued him from the hands of Alambayana. They attacked the culprits and bit them with vengeance. The bodies of Alambayana and his companions soon started rotting under the effect of venom. But kind as Bhuuridatta was, he forgave his captors and arranged for medicines that revived and cured them. Bhuuridatta's fortitude pleased Sakka, the king of Gods, and he gave the pious snake his whole-hearted blessings.

02 Bamboo's Father

Once there lived a famous teacher who had many disciples. One of them was a great animal lover and wanted to keep every animal as his pet. Once he saw a small poisonous snake and kept it as a pet in a bamboo cage. The other disciples called the snake "Bamboo" and his keeper, "Bamboo's Father".

When the teacher came to know about Bamboo, he told Bamboo's Father that it would be dangerous to keep the snake as pet and advised him to let it go. But Bamboo's Father did not listen to his teacher and thought that he knew better. One day, the teacher sent his disciples on a trip to collect fruits. Bamboo's Father also accompanied them leaving the snake at home. They returned after several days. Realising that Bamboo would be hungry, he opened the bamboo cage to feed the snake. But the moment he opened it, Bamboo bit him hard. Writhing in pain, he recalled his teacher's advice. But alas! It was too late and he died.

03 The Crab and the Elephant

Once upon a time there lived a giant golden crab in a lake in the Himalayas. He used to eat the elephants who came to the lake to drink water. Realising that the place was no longer safe for them, all the other elephants except the Bodhisattva and his wife left the place. Feeling thirsty the elephant went to the lake. Having drunk to his fill, he was about to leave the lake when the golden crab caught the Bodhisattva. Hearing his painful cries, his wife decided to help her husband and risking her life came up to the crab. She started flattering the crab by praising his mighty strength and majestic look. The foolish crab got carried away with her words and loosened his grip on the Bodhisattva. Releasing himself, the Bodhisattva at once gave a war cry and crushed the crab with his heavy paws.

04 Do-gooder Expresses Her desire to Do Social Work

Magha the wise had four wives. The eldest wife was Do-gooder and the others were known as Beauty, Happy and Well-born. Among them Do-gooder was the wisest and wanted to serve society by doing some good work. During that time Magha and his fellow villagers were building a big roadside inn. The lady decided to take part in the project. But she knew that the men wouldn't be open to the idea of a woman working with them. So she didn't approach them directly and instead made friends with the head of the project. After a few days, the woman said to the head, "Sir, please tell me how I can be of use in your project. I really want to make a contribution to this noble work." The head thought for a while and said, "I have a plan. If it clicks then I am sure the men will relent and let you work with them." He secretly constructed a sturdy beam that would help to hold the roof together and asked the woman to hide it until it dried and hardened and was fit to be used.

05 Do-gooder Joins the Men in building the Inn

The men constructing the inn needed a strong beam to make the roof of the inn. The head told them, "Friends, ithink we need an old but strong beam which we can get in any of our houses." The villagers went from door to door but no one had a spare beam. At last they came to Magha's house. Do-gooder showed them the beam that the head had prepared and it was perfect for the inn. Delighted, the men offered to pay her well. Seeing the right opportunity to place her proposal, Do-gooder said, "I can give you this beam only if you let me join the project." The men didn't like the proposal, as it was not customary for the women to take part in any kind of public work. So they went back to their head and reported what had happened. The head said, "Why don't you want women to work with you? They are part of everything that happens in this world. If we involve them in our project, it will be more successful and complete." At last the men agreed and Do-gooder became a part of the noble project.

06 Sweet and Bitter Figs

Once upon a time Benares was ruled by a very just and noble king. To find out how contented his subjects were, the king once disguised himself as an ordinary man and travelled the entire kingdom. He went to different towns and finally he came to the Himalayas where the Bodhisattva lived as an ascetic. The king was hungry and asked the Bodhisattva for food. The Bodhisattva offered him some ripe figs, which the king found to be surprisingly sweet and tasty. Curious, he asked the Bodhisattva how this was possible. "The sweetness in the figs shows the prosperity and joy in your kingdom and the credit for it goes to you, my king," said the Bodhisattva. The king returned to his palace and to test the Bodhisattva's words, ruled unjustly for a while and went back to the Bodhisattva to taste the figs. This time he found that the figs had become bitter.

07 The Lotus Stalk

The Bodhisattva was once born into a renowned family of scholars with six siblings. After his parents' death, he left the luxuries of worldly life and decided to live in the forest as an ascetic. His brothers and sisters along with their servant also accompanied him to the forest. They strictly observed a vow to meet only on every fifth day of the week for the Bodhisattva's discourse and to spend the rest of their time in complete meditation and silence. The ascetics used to eat lotus stalks, which they picked from the lake. Sakka, the king of gods, observed the ascetics and decided to test the Bodhisattva's patience. For four consecutive days, Sakka stole the lotus stalks, the only meal the ascetics had in a day. But the Bodhisattva remained calm and continued with his meditation. On the fifth day, while giving his discourse, the Bodhisattva became weak, as he was starving. But instead of cursing or trying to catch the thief, the ascetics prayed together for the thief's well-being. This made Sakka feel guilty and ashamed. He appeared before the Bodhisattva and confessed his sin.

08 The King Who Learnt a Lesson from a Monkey

Once, the king of a large kingdom made up his mind to attack a small neighbouring state. He gathered his entire army and set out to attack. When it grew dark, the king ordered his soldiers to camp in the forest. They fed their horses with buckets full of peas. A monkey was observing the horses eating. The moment he thought no one was looking, he jumped down from the tree, picked up a handful of peas and climbed up again. As the monkey sat eating, one of the peas slipped from his hand and fell on the ground. He at once dropped the rest of the peas and jumped down to pick up the fallen pea. But alas, when he went up, he realised what he had done for he had just one pea to eat. The king had been watching the monkey and thought, "I'll not be foolish like this monkey and lose my men in battle for the sake of a small state." He gave up his plan for conquest and calling together his army, marched back home.

09 King Sudhana and Manohara

Once there were two kings, Sudhana and Manohara, who reigned over two separate kingdoms. Sudhana's kingdom prospered for he was a just and benevolent ruler. Moreover, his kingdom was blessed by the presence of the naga serpent, Janmacitraka. Manohara's subjects suffered for he was a ruthless king. They started leaving his kingdom to settle in Sudhana's kingdom. When King Manohara came to know about Janmacitraka, he decided to bring the naga serpent to his kingdom with the help of the enchanting spells of a snake charmer. Janmacitraka came to know about King Manohara's plan and with the help of Halaka, a hunter who happened to be his friend, got the snake charmer killed. Thus Janmacitraka continued to live in King Sudhana's kingdom and Halaka was rewarded with lot of gifts.

10 Ghata: The Virtuous King

The Bodhisattva was once born as Ghata, the king of Benaras. He was a very just king. One day King Ghata saw one of his ministers misbehaving with a woman. He was furious and banished the minister from his kingdom. The wicked minister went to Vanka, the king of a neighbouring state and planned to take revenge. He persuaded King Vanka to attack the kingdom of Benaras. King Ghata lost the battle and was taken prisoner. One day, while King Vanka was taking a round of the prison, he saw Ghata meditating peacefully in his cell. Unable to hold back his curiosity, King Vanka went up to Ghata and asked, "How could you remain so cool and peaceful when you are in prison?" At this Ghata smiled and said, "To grieve is in vain. Grief cannot heal the sorrow of the past and gives no hope for the future. So why should I allow it to master me?" Ghata's words impressed King Vanka and he not only set him free, but also restored Ghata's kingdom.

11 Pindola Bharadvaja

Once a holy man lived in the kingdom of Rajagaha. His name was Pindola Bharadvaja. One day, a proud merchant visited the kingdom and put forward a challenge to the holy men with the intention to make fun of them and insult them in public. He placed a sandalwood bowl on top of a high pole, which was beyond anybody's reach and asked the holy men to bring it down to prove their powers. All the holy men who were present were unable to meet the challenge and the merchant took the opportunity to ridicule and insult them. Pindola Bharadvaja was also present and when he saw that no one was ready to accept the challenge, he came forward and offered to try his powers. Pindola flew up like a bird, reached the top of the pole and brought the sandalwood bowl down to the utter amazement of all the spectators. The merchant was ashamed of himself and left the place immediately.

12 A Tale of Consciousness

The Bodhisattva was once born as the son of a learned Brahmin and was sent to a teacher for education as was the custom in those days. To test his students, the teacher lamented his own poverty and asked his students to steal for him. He said, "The only way to become rich and get rid of poverty in a short time is to steal." All the students, except the Bodhisattva, began planning how and what they were going to steal for their teacher. The Bodhisattva sat with downcast eyes feeling ashamed of what was going on. Seeing him, his teacher came up to him and accused him of being indifferent to his plight. At this, the Bodhisattva humbly replied that he sympathises with him and was willing to do anything to help. But his conscience forbade him to steal as it was morally wrong. The teacher was pleased with his reply and hugged him saying, "Well said, my son! You're indeed a virtuous soul and have passed my test."

13 Bitterness

The Bodhisattva was once born as an ascetic. In the course of his wanderings, he came to Benaras and was welcomed as the king's royal guest for the rainy season. He stayed in the royal park and spent his time in meditation. The king had an ill-natured son named Dutthakumara. The king tried to modify him but failed. So he requested the Bodhisattva to help him.

One day, the ascetic and the prince were strolling in the royal garden. The ascetic asked him to taste the leaf of a nearby plant. The moment the prince tasted the leaf, he spat it out as it was bitter. Seeing this the Bodhisattva said, "It's the leaf of a young plant, but yet it's so bitter. Imagine how bitter it would taste when the tree grows up." Hearing him, the young prince realised what the Bodhisattva meant and from that day onwards he tried to mend his ways.

14 The Meditating Security Guard

The Bodhisattva was once born into a royal family. Early in life he got bored with worldly life and became a hermit. One day, while he was on his way through the village to collect alms, he joined a caravan and spent the night with them. The hermit used to reach a state of divine knowledge if he kept walking at night. So, while the others were sleeping, the hermit kept awake and walking. Late in the night, some robbers came up to the caravan. But when they saw the hermit walking up and down, they mistook him for a security guard and dropping their weapons, ran away. In the morning when the others woke up and saw the weapons left behind by the robbers, they were alarmed and went to the hermit to ask if he had seen the thieves. "Weren't you afraid?" asked one of them. The hermit smiled and said, "I've nothing to lose. All I have is love and compassion, which no one can take away. So why should I fear?" Everyone was impressed with the hermit's words and realised what true wealth was.

15 The King Orders the Death of Stray Dogs

Once upon a time, the king of Benaras had a majestic chariot, which had beautiful hand-worked leather straps. One day the king went to his royal garden riding on his chariot and returned late at night leaving the chariot outside in the porch. That night it rained heavily and the leather got totally soaked. It started giving off a smell that attracted the palace dogs and together they chewed up the wet leather straps with great relish. The next morning when the king found that the straps had been chewed up, he was very angry and ordered his men to catch the culprits. The servants who were in charge of the dogs knew the truth. But fearing the wrath of the king, they falsely informed him that some stray dogs had sneaked into the compound and had eaten the leather straps. The king was so enraged that he ordered the death of every stray dog in the city of Benaras.

16 Dog King Silver Seeks Justice for the Stray Dogs

The king's decree saw a massive slaughter of dogs in the city of Benaras. The few who escaped the killing hid in the cemetery outside the city and reported the unfortunate incident to their leader King Silver. King Silver was an average-sized dog with silver fur, pointed ears and dark sparkling eyes, which reflected the sharpness of his mind. He was wise and pious

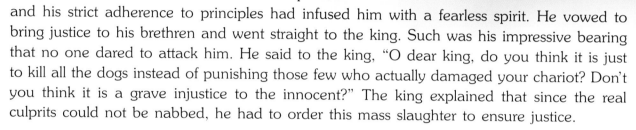

and his strict adherence to principles had infused him with a fearless spirit. He vowed to bring justice to his brethren and went straight to the king. Such was his impressive bearing that no one dared to attack him. He said to the king, "O dear king, do you think it is just to kill all the dogs instead of punishing those few who actually damaged your chariot? Don't you think it is a grave injustice to the innocent?" The king explained that since the real culprits could not be nabbed, he had to order this mass slaughter to ensure justice.

17 Dog King Silver Teaches the King to Be Just

King Silver laughed at the explanation the king gave for his ruthless slaughter of the dogs. "Your majesty, these words speak nothing about your reputation as a righteous king. May I ask you a question? Have you made sure that all the guilty dogs are dead?" The king now felt a bit uncomfortable. He stammered, "No… umm…actually my high-breed dogs have been spared." Then King Silver said, "Your action speaks of your prejudice against stray dogs which is not expected from a righteous king like you. If you had thought carefully you would realise that no stray dog would dare enter your guarded premises. Instead, it is more likely that some palace dogs are responsible for this damage." The dog's argument made perfect sense to the king and he realised he had been rash and unjust. He called all his dogs and gave them buttermilk and grass to eat. After eating the mixture, the dogs vomited parts of undigested leather. King Silver then told the shame-faced king, "O king, I don't wish death for your dogs. But in future, please be just in your decisions."

18 Prince Temiya Decides to Become an Ascetic

The Bodhisattva was once born as Temiya, the prince of Varanasi. His father was so happy at his birth that he offered to fulfill any wish the queen might have. The queen, however, requested the king to save the promise for the future. As a child, the prince used to travel across the kingdom to learn the responsibilities of a ruler, and his tender heart was touched by the harsh actions his father had to take against criminals. Temiya realised that once he ascended the throne, he too would have to be cruel. This thought kept troubling him until one night God appeared to him and said, "My dear, if you really don't want to be the king then pretend to be crippled and mute." The next morning, following God's advice, Temiya started acting like a disabled person. His parents were devastated and put him under the best of medication. But still the condition of the prince didn't improve.

19 Prince Temiya Turns Ascetic

The royal priest considered Prince Temiya's sudden illness a bad omen for the kingdom and advised the king to get rid of him. With a heavy heart, the king ordered his son's execution. When the news reached the queen, she came running. "O my lord! How can you be so harsh on your own son?" cried she. But the king had no choice and refused to listen. The queen fell at his feet and said, "Then spare my son's life for seven days. Grant this request of mine as you had promised earlier." The king relented and the prince was given seven more days to live. During this time, the queen ceaselessly begged Temiya to speak but he remained mute. When finally Temiya was brought to the execution ground, he hauled up the executioner's chariot and said to the bewildered executioner, "My friend, I am all right. Actually I want to be an ascetic instead of a king." Saying these words, Prince Temiya left for the jungle.

20 Heaven Dweller

The Bodhisattva, living amidst all the comforts of heaven was always keen to help those suffering on earth. Angadinna, the king of Videha, nursed a false notion that there was no afterlife and indulged in immoral acts fearing no retribution. The Bodhisattva noted that this otherwise good king had gone astray due to bad companions. Their words had made the king lose interest in charity and religion. He came down to earth to give him advice and recite sermons. The king was amazed to see the resplendent beauty of the Bodhisattva and realised that, contrary to his belief, there existed a life after death during which a person's actions were judged and punished or rewarded accordingly.

21 The Wolf Who Broke His Fast

Once upon a time, a wolf lived in a rocky place near the Ganges. One monsoon the water overflowed and flooded the surrounding land. The wolf got trapped within the rocks and seeing no other way to escape the turbulent waters he cried, "O God, please help me out of this trouble. I promise I'll keep a fast today and refrain from eating meat." Hearing him, Sakka decided to test the strength of his promise. Transforming himself to a goat he appeared in front of the wolf. The wolf felt greedy and forgetting all about his promise went after him hoping to have a great feast. He went on chasing him but no matter how fast he ran, always found the goat a little ahead of him. At last the wolf gave up. "Thank God that I couldn't catch him, else my promise would have been broken," said he. Sakka resumed his normal self and chided the wolf for his weakness. "You have no firmness of character. A promise which is forgotten at the slightest temptation is not a promise at all."

22 Salty Liquor

Once upon a time, a tavern owner in Benaras had a foolish bartender working for him. One afternoon, the tavern owner went to bathe in the river leaving the tavern in charge of the bartender. The bartender was very happy to help his master. He had always wondered why most customers ate a little bit of salt after drinking their liquor but never asked the real reason, lest it should show his ignorance. He had no idea that the salt helped to reduce the aftereffect of liquor. Instead, he thought that the salt was needed for good taste. "Why don't we serve drink with salt in it? I am sure our customers will like it and our profits will increase," thought he. So he added salt into the drink and served it to the customers. But, to his surprise, all of them spat out the drink, yelled at him and went to another tavern. When the owner returned, he saw his tavern empty and all his liquor ruined.

23 Ingratitude

Once upon a time there lived two merchant friends, one in Benaras and the other in the countryside. One day, the country merchant sent a large caravan of five hundred carts loaded with a large quantity of goods to his friend in the city. The city merchant was very pleased and invited the carriers to stay in his own home. He was very courteous to them and made sure that they got the best price for the goods they had brought for sale. A few months later, the city merchant sent a caravan of five hundred carts to the countryside. But the country merchant took the gifts from them and sent them away without offering any kind of assistance. They went to the market and traded their goods on their own and then returned to Benaras. Before long, the country merchant again sent his caravan to Benaras. But this time, the men working for the Benaras merchant took them to a deserted place outside the city and robbed them off all their belongings. The terrified men ran back to their village.

24 The Ominous Sounds

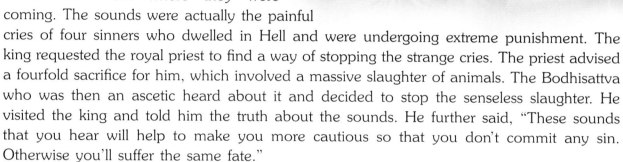

Once upon a time, a king of Benaras used to hear strange sounds at night. After listening hard, he could make out that these sounds were like the four syllables du, sa, na, so. He felt frightened as he didn't know what those sounds meant and from where they were coming. The sounds were actually the painful cries of four sinners who dwelled in Hell and were undergoing extreme punishment. The king requested the royal priest to find a way of stopping the strange cries. The priest advised a fourfold sacrifice for him, which involved a massive slaughter of animals. The Bodhisattva who was then an ascetic heard about it and decided to stop the senseless slaughter. He visited the king and told him the truth about the sounds. He further said, "These sounds that you hear will help to make you more cautious so that you don't commit any sin. Otherwise you'll suffer the same fate."

25 The Holy Man Who Tried to Be Too Holy

Once, the Bodhisattva lived in a period when men believed that the only way to remove all kinds of suffering from one's mind was to make one's body suffer. It might sound strange but during that period it was believed that the holiest souls were the ones who had tortured their bodies the most. Accordingly the Bodhisattva, too, gave up all luxuries and led a frugal life. He even discarded basic comforts and spent his life under a tree braving rough weather. The sun scorched his body and winter cracked his skin. Thus he reached the last days of his life. Then, just as he was about to breathe his last, he saw a vision of himself reborn in a hellish world. He realised that even after leading such a hard life he had not obtained peace of mind. So he renounced his false belief and after his death was reborn in Heaven.

26 Bhaddasala, the Tree Deity

Once, King Brahmadatta of Benaras wished to build an unique palace supported only on one column. All his carpenters went around looking for a tree with a trunk strong enough to hold a palace. They spotted a giant sal tree in the royal garden and prepared to cut it down. Now, there resided in the tree a sprite named Bhaddasala who was actually the Bodhisattva. When he saw the preparations he felt distressed, as he knew that when the carpenters felled the tree, all the surrounding, trees would also get damaged. So, at midnight, the tree sprite visited the king and requested him not to cut down the tree. When the king turned down his request saying that he was determined to build the palace, Bhaddasala asked him to cut the tree part by part so that while falling it would not farm the nearby trees. Bhaddasala's words aroused compassion in the king's heart and he dropped his plan to make the unique palace.

27 Sakka Plans to Tempt Noble Kassapa

Once the Bodhisattva was born as Kassapa, the son of a royal chaplain. Kassapa and the king's son were childhood friends and had been students of the same teacher. When the prince ascended the throne, Kassapa being disinterested in worldly life, became an ascetic and through meditation started acquiring supernatural power. Sakka, the king of gods, became scared of his increasing power and decided to curb it. He knew this could only be done by distracting the man from the path of virtue. Thus, one night Sakka appeared in front of the king and asked him to persuade Kassapa into killing animals. "Do what I say and one day you'll rule over the whole of India," said Sakka. The king agreed and sent for Kassapa, but the latter having already learned about the plan, refused to meet him.

28 Noble Kassapa Conquers Temptation

Sakka met the king again and advised him to tell Kassapa that if Kassapa complied, the king would give him his daughter Candavadi in marriage. This time the king personally met Kassapa taking his daughter along with him and gave him his proposal. Kassapa became fascinated with the princess' beauty and agreed to do as told. Forgetting all about his principles, Kassapa started slaying animals until a royal elephant gave a heart-wrenching cry which was joined by the cries of other animals. Their screams filled his heart with remorse and he felt ashamed of what he had done. "Alas, after all these years of meditation how could I give up my sense of right and wrong and surrender myself to a trivial passion?" cried he. He chastised the king for being so hungry for power and went back to his ascetic life.

29 Gain

Once upon a time, Buddha was born as a famous teacher of the Vedas. Some five hundred pupils used to take lessons under him. One day, one of his students who still could not conquer his desire for worldly life asked his teacher, "O holy being, how can one gain happiness in this world? What does an ascetic gain at the end of his life?" Buddha smiled and said, "My dear, at the end of his life an ascetic feels happy to have acquired knowledge and wisdom and receives the blessing of God. In this world of fools where men have forgotten the path of virtue, the man who slanders, changes colours with changing situations and talks evil things succeeds in gaining material prosperity. But at the end of this mortal life he suffers endless torture in hell." His words had a deep impression on the student and he decided to become an ascetic.

30 The Unruly Master

Once in a forest lived an ascetic who had a pet elephant whom he had reared up since it was just a baby. But all his fellow hermits felt it was risky to have a wild elephant as a pet. One day the Bodhisattva, who was his teacher, told him, "My son, it was kind of you to rear this motherless elephant. But now that he has grown up and is strong enough to fend for himself, I advice you to leave him on his own. Since we stay in the forest, the elephant is well acquainted with the wild. He may drop his benign nature and behave like a wild elephant at any moment." But the stubborn ascetic laughed away his teacher's advice. One day all hermits were away in a nearby village when the elephant was seized with frenzy. His master was the only one present in the forest and in a fit of madness, the elephant killed him.

31 Prince Hatthipala

Long time ago, a childless king called Esukari ruled over Benaras. His chaplain came to know about a tree deity who had the power to give sons to the childless and went to request him to grant a son to King Esukari. But the deity said it was not under his power to do so. Instead, he would give four sons to the chaplain, who would become ascetics in their youth. In due course four sons were born to the chaplain and were named Hatthipala, Gopala, Assapala and Ajapala. True to the prediction, Hatthipala left his home in his youth and his brothers too joined him, ignoring all the temptations of worldly life. Later on, their parents too joined them. King Esukari decided to seize all their possessions but his queen made him see the sin of grabbing other people's property. Together they gave up their royal life and joined Hatthipala.

Contents

The Story of the Month: The Ungrateful Son

September

The Ungrateful Son

01 The Ungrateful Son

Once upon a time in a certain village near Kasi there lived a young man named Vasitthaka. As the only breadwinner of the house it was Vasitthaka's responsibility to look after the family and he carried out his duties well. But everything changed after he got married. His wife was selfish and didn't like to have her old in-laws in the house. Things got worse after the death of Vasitthaka's mother. The woman hated her father-in-law as he was very old and feeble and was totally dependant on his son. Every day she urged her husband to drive his father away. "It is impossible for me to stay with your father under the same roof. He is forever picking fights with me. I don't know why he doesn't like me. And yet I always have to look after his needs. But now enough is enough. I can't take it any more. If your father has no other place to go then...well, take him to a cemetery, dig a pit, poison him and bury him there. In any case, he will die before long. So it won't be a bad idea if we leave him there," the wicked woman suggested. And this she continued to say day after day till she finally had her way

and the young man decided to follow her advice. Now, while the two were discussing their wicked plans, Vasitthaka's seven-year-old son overheard everything. Wise as he was the little kid realised that his mother had totally corrupted his father's mind and decided to stop his father from committing the heinous crime. Next morning, when his grandfather got up on the cart to go out with Vasitthaka, his little grandson too went and sat beside him. Seeing no other option, Vasitthaka set out on his journey taking both his son and father along. On reaching the cemetery, he got down from the cart and went to the remotest corner of the cemetery. His son quietly followed him. As soon as he started digging up the ground, the boy came up to him and asked, "Why are you digging, Father?" "Oh son, your grandfather is very old and in pain. It is better to die than suffer so much. So I'll give him some poison to drink and then bury him here to lie in peace," explained Vasitthaka. Hearing this, the little boy took another shovel and started digging up the ground. "What are you doing, my lad?" asked Vashittaka, surprised. "O Father! One day you too will reach this stage. Then I'll have to poison you and bury you here to let you lie in peace," answered the boy. "Lad! You are planning to murder your own father?" cried Vasitthaka, horrified. "Why not, Father? If, to appease my mother, you can murder your own father who all through his life showered you with so much love and care, then how can you expect me to behave otherwise?" His words stunned Vasitthaka and he realised what a grave mistake he was going to make. He took both his son and his father in his arms and returned home.

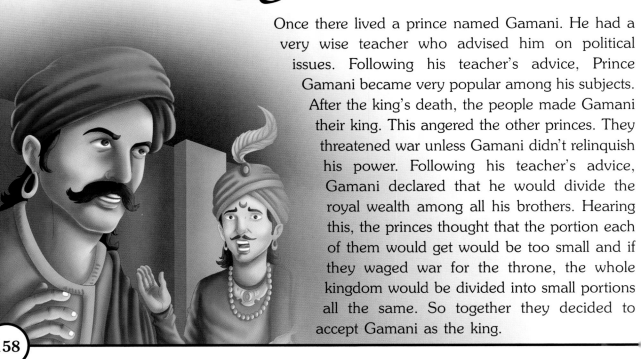

02 The Footprint Reader

Once the Bodhisattva was born as the son of a *yakshni* and had the special power to read the footprints of any creature, even if the footprints were twelve years old. Seeing his extraordinary power, the king of Benaras made him his minister. One day, the king and his chaplain stole some public money and hid it in a tank. When the theft was discovered, the king and his chaplain pretended to be innocent and ordered the Bodhisattva to find the thieves. Since the Bodhisattva could read the footprints of any person, he soon found the money and also found out who the thieves were. "Do tell us the names of the guilty," pleaded the public with the Bodhisattva. After much persuasion, the Bodhisattva revealed the identity of the thieves. The people were infuriated and banished the dishonest king and his chaplain from the kingdom. Soon the Bodhisattva was crowned the king and the kingdom of Benaras prospered under him.

03 A Wise Teacher

Once there lived a prince named Gamani. He had a very wise teacher who advised him on political issues. Following his teacher's advice, Prince Gamani became very popular among his subjects. After the king's death, the people made Gamani their king. This angered the other princes. They threatened war unless Gamani didn't relinquish his power. Following his teacher's advice, Gamani declared that he would divide the royal wealth among all his brothers. Hearing this, the princes thought that the portion each of them would get would be too small and if they waged war for the throne, the whole kingdom would be divided into small portions all the same. So together they decided to accept Gamani as the king.

04 Two Otters and a Wolf

Once there lived a wolf and his wife. One day, the wife wanted to eat fresh fish and said, "It's been a long time we ate fresh fish." So the wolf went to the river to fetch some. There he met two otters catching fish. They caught sight of a big fish and both pounced on it. One otter said, "Let's divide the fish in two parts." Soon they started quarrelling as both of them wanted to have the bigger part with the head. The wolf heard them and offered to help them divide the fish. He cut off the tail and gave it to one and the head to the other. Taking the big middle part he ran away saying, "You can eat the head and the tail without quarrelling." The otters stood gaping at each other. They had nothing to do but lament the loss. The wolf went to his wife and said, "I had the fish as a reward for settling the quarrel between two otters." His wife smiled and happily ate the fish.

05 The Foolish Disciple

The Bodhisattva was once born into a Brahmin family and later grew up to be a teacher. He had many disciples among whom was a very foolish but devoted youth who had a habit of saying all the wrong things. With a hope to improve him, the Bodhisattva asked him to tell him whatever he saw or did every day.

One day, while walking the youth came upon a snake. When he told the Bodhisattva about it, he asked, "How does the snake look?" The student thought for a while and said, "It looks exactly like the handle of a plough." The Bodhisattva found the expression good. But when the disciple went on to compare the look of a plough handle to that of an elephant, a sugarcane plant, molasses and even curd and milk, the Bodhisattva realised that his disciple was indeed foolish and could never become as intelligent as the others.

06 Ayogriha

Once the Bodhisattva was born as Prince Ayogriha. Before his birth, many sons had been born to the royal family but had died after birth due to the spell of some evil spirits. So when Ayogriha was born, the king performed many religious rites to ward off the threat. These steps combined with the innate virtue of the child protected him from all harm and he grew up to be a strong and noble man. Once during the time of the Kaumudi festival ,the young prince went forth to see the celebrations. After observing for a while, he came to the conclusion that all this celebration was meaningless as death, disease and old age waited for all. He lost interest in the festival and later turned ascetic in order to conquer the fear of death and attain true happiness through good deeds and meditation.

07 The King Who Knew the Language of Animals

Once a king saved the life of a serpent and in turn the serpent gifted him the power to understand the language of animals provided he kept it a secret, else he would have to die. One day when he was sitting with his queen in the garden, he heard an ant speak about a piece of sweet and he smiled as he listened. Seeing him smile, the queen pressed him to tell her the reason even though the king warned her of the consequence. Just as the king was about to reveal his secret, a lightning flashed and he heard a heavenly voice say, "O king, why should you sacrifice your life for someone who doesn't value yours?" The king thought over the words and told his queen that he would tell her the secret only if she took a hundred lashes on her back. The queen agreed, but after three lashes was unable to bear the pain and refused to take any more. The king accused his wife of being selfish for she had insisted on knowing his secret at the cost of his life. The queen realised her mistake and promised never to ask the king about his secret.

08 Sariputta

Sariputta was one of the chief disciples of Buddha. One night, when Sariputta was sitting under a tree in deep meditation, his shaven head shining in the moonlight, a Yaksha who was flying above noticed him. He thought, "Aha! This monk seems to be in deep meditation. Let me break his concentration with a hard blow on his shiny head." So the Yaksha flew down closer to the monk's head and gave a powerful blow. Startled, the monk looked around. Then he looked up to see if a coconut had fallen on his head. His eyes fell on the flying Yaksha and closing his eyes, he continued with his meditation. The Yaksha was surprised to see that the blow, which was strong enough to crush a mountain, could do no harm to the monk. Impressed, he came down and fell at the monk's feet seeking forgiveness.

09 Dirty Water

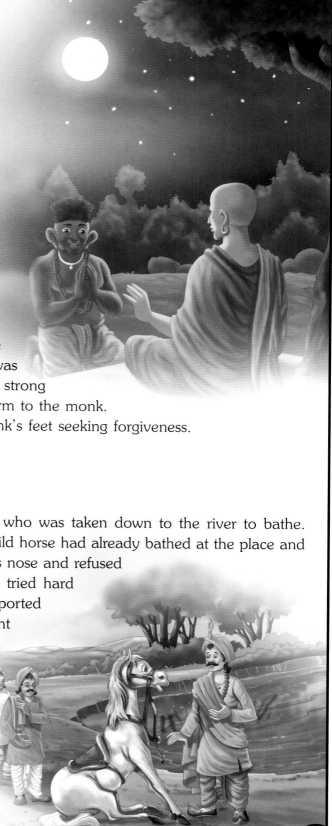

Once upon a time there was a royal horse who was taken down to the river to bathe. Before the grooms reached the river, a dirty wild horse had already bathed at the place and made it dirty. So the royal horse turned up his nose and refused to be washed in the dirty water. The grooms tried hard to take him into the water, but failed. They reported the matter to the king who had an intelligent minister known for his understanding of animals. The king sent him to find out why the horse had not taken its bath.

Having learnt about the incident, the minister instructed the grooms to take the horse to a clean bathing place. This time the horse was washed without any trouble. The minister went back to the king and explained the matter. The king was very pleased and awarded him handsomely.

10 The Ungrateful Husband

Once upon a time, a prince and his wife were returning after a long journey. On the way back, they felt very hungry and were looking for something to eat. Some hunters, who were passing by, gave them a roasted lizard to eat. But while his wife was away fetching water, the prince ate the whole lizard and when she came back said that the lizard had run away leaving only its tail in his hand. Later, the prince became the king, but he did not give his wife her due honour although she was the queen. The Bodhisattva, who happened to be the king's minister, saw the injustice and reminded the king how he had wronged her before. The king realised that he had been unfair to his dutiful wife and gave her the status she deserved.

11 The Geese and the Greedy Crow

Once there lived a crow in a tree on the riverbank. Every day the crow fed on the river fish but was never satisfied. "Wish I could have the best of the fish all for myself," the crow often thought. One day a fisherman came to fish in the river and caught a few very big fish in his net. Seeing the catch, the crow felt greedy and when a fish fell out of the fisherman's basket, it flew down and gobbled it up. Yet still he was unhappy and wanted more. Suddenly his eyes fell on two golden geese flying over the river. "Oh! How beautiful they look. Must be eating real good food unlike me," thought the crow and flew up to the geese. "What do you eat to look so beautiful?" enquired the crow. The geese smiled and said, "It's not food but character that makes you good to look at." But the crow was too greedy to follow these words.

12 The Little Bird that Saved the Forest

Once a powerful fire engulfed the entire forest and all animals and birds started running here and there to save their lives. The Bodhisattva, who was born as a little bird, managed to escape. But after saving himself from the fire, he thought of his parents, brothers and sisters who were sure to be engulfed by the raging flames and became anxious to save them. The little bird flew to a nearby river and diving inside, soaked himself all over. Then he flew back to the burning forest, gathered all the energy in his tiny body and shook his wings so that the droplets fell on the flames. Repeatedly the bird went back and forth in his effort to douse the fire showing no signs of fear or tiredness. The gods in heaven were so touched by the little bird's concern that the gates of Heaven opened and heavy rain started pouring. The fire was put out and everyone was saved.

13 Impartiality

Once, the Bodhisattva was born as Brahmadatta, the king of Benaras. In the neighbouring kingdom there ruled Mallika, another famous king. One day, both of them disguised themselves and roamed the streets to make sure no injustice was happening in their kingdom. Both came upon a narrow street and their chariots stood face to face with each other. The chariot drivers started arguing who should go forward first. None of them was ready to let the other pass. Each driver sang the praises of his own master. As they argued, they discovered that Mallika was good to the good and bad to the bad people, while Brahmadatta was good to both the good and the bad. So finally Mallika's chariot driver accepted Brahmadatta as superior to Mallika and made way for the latter's chariot.

14 The Young Monk Who Saved the Ants

Once the Bodhisattva was born as a young monk in a forest deep in the mountains. He was the disciple of an old monk who used to be in deep meditation all the time. One day, in his meditation he came to know that the young monk would die in another eight days. So he called him and told him to go and meet his parents. The young monk was very happy and went down the mountains to his village. He stopped to drink some water from a stream and saw an anthill inside a cave nearby. The water in the stream was rising and he feared the ants might all drown. He quickly built a protective wall at the mouth of the cave, which stopped the water from going inside, and so the ants were saved. Due to this good deed the gods granted him a long and happy life and the old monk was very happy for him.

15 The Chameleon Who Saved a Tree

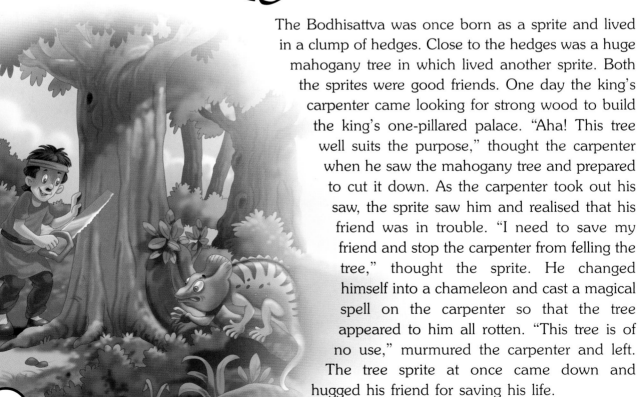

The Bodhisattva was once born as a sprite and lived in a clump of hedges. Close to the hedges was a huge mahogany tree in which lived another sprite. Both the sprites were good friends. One day the king's carpenter came looking for strong wood to build the king's one-pillared palace. "Aha! This tree well suits the purpose," thought the carpenter when he saw the mahogany tree and prepared to cut it down. As the carpenter took out his saw, the sprite saw him and realised that his friend was in trouble. "I need to save my friend and stop the carpenter from felling the tree," thought the sprite. He changed himself into a chameleon and cast a magical spell on the carpenter so that the tree appeared to him all rotten. "This tree is of no use," murmured the carpenter and left. The tree sprite at once came down and hugged his friend for saving his life.

16 The Lizard

The Bodhisattva was once born as a forest lizard. A wicked ascetic built a hut of leaves in the forest where the lizard lived and started living there. One day, the lizard crawled into the hut of the ascetic and seeing him meditating, paid his respects to him. From then on he started visiting the ascetic regularly. One day, the ascetic had a tasty meal prepared with lizard meat in the house of one of the villagers and decided to kill the forest lizard for another meal. The next day the ascetic made the necessary arrangements and as soon as the lizard came into his hut, threw his staff at him. The wise lizard turned aside swiftly and the staff bounced off the wall and hit hard on the ascetic's head. "Ouch…" cried the ascetic in pain and fell down unconscious in a pool of blood.

17 The Little Boy Who Saved the Ants

A large tree once stood on the bank of a stream. At the foot of this tree, was a large anthill. During one monsoon, the water level in the stream kept on rising. The ants got panicky and did not know what to do to save themselves from drowning.

So they decided to leave the place. Some of them took the eggs while some took the other provisions and started moving out of their colony .The Bodhisattva, born as a little boy, was sitting near the stream, watching these ants struggling to save themselves. He felt pity for them and placed a big leaf across the stream to make it look like a bridge. When the ants saw it they used it to cross over to the other bank. Thus the whole colony of ants was saved and they thanked the little boy for his kindness.

18 The Grateful Elephant

Near a forest close to Benaras lived a group of carpenters who earned their livelihood by building houses. Every day the carpenters would go to the forest to cut wood. In that same forest lived a noble elephant. One day, the elephant stepped on a splinter and it pierced his foot. The foot swelled up and festered. Unable to bear the pain the elephant went trumpeting through the forest seeking help. Suddenly, his eyes fell on the carpenters busy felling trees. "Huuuooo!" trumpeted the elephant and lay down on the ground. Amazed at the elephant's behaviour, the carpenters rushed to see what the matter was. "Look! His foot is festering," pointed out one of the carpenters. They pulled out the splinter and bandaged the elephant's wound. Filled with gratitude, the elephant offered to help the carpenters in their work. From then on the elephant pulled up trees and rolled logs for them. The carpenters in turn fed the elephant and enjoyed his service.

19 Wastefulness

Once there lived a very rich man who did not know the value of money. He lived such a wasteful life that the drainage pipe coming out of his house used to be full of rice grains. At that time, the Bodhisattva was a monk living next to the rich man. He was shocked to see the grains of rice coming out of the rich man's drain. Every day he made it a point to

collect the rice from the pipe, wash and dry it nicely and store it for future use. In this way, he accumulated a large quantity of rice. After some time, the rich man met with a mishap and lost all his wealth. He became so poor that he had to beg for food. One day, while begging, the rich man and his wife came to the monk's house. He gave them the same rice, which he had accumulated for years and told them where he had found it. The rich man and his wife bowed their heads in shame for their wastefulness.

20 Kalanduka, the Wicked Servant

The treasurer of Benaras had a dishonest servant named Kalanduka. Though his master treated him well, Kalanduka always looked for a chance to rob his master. "I have to steal this man's money and escape as soon as possible," Kalanduka often thought. One day when his master was away, he stole all the money and ran away. He went to a border town and married a merchant's daughter. Meanwhile, his master returned and feeling greatly annoyed sent his parrot to search for Kalanduka . The parrot flew over many villages and at last spotted a house where he saw a man ill-treating his wife. The parrot at once recognised Kalanduka and flew to inform his master. "Bring that imposter to me," the treasurer ordered his servants. Kalanduka was brought before his master. "Forgive me, my lord. I'll never deceive you again," pleaded Kalanduka. "You don't deserve any mercy," said the treasurer and made him a slave again.

21 Impatience

A king's minister was once passing with his caravan through a narrow muddy road to his village estate. On the way he came across a bullock cart, which stood stuck in the mud and blocked the way. The carter was trying in vain to pull out the wheels of the cart. "Get out of my way," shouted the proud minister. "Sir, my cart is stuck in the mud. You'll have to wait till I pull out the wheels," said the carter politely. Furious, the minister picked up a huge stone and threw it at the bullock cart. But alas, instead of hitting the cart, the stone hit the chain of his own caravan and bouncing back, hit the minister's forehead. Writhing in pain, the minister went and complained about the carter to the king who without any enquiry ordered the carter to be punished. But the Bodhisattva, who was the chief judge, came to know the truth and changed the order.

22 The Wicked Chameleon

The Bodhisattva was once born as the leader of the iguanas and lived with his family in the forest. He had a young son who made friends with a chameleon. The Bodhisattva did not approve of this and often warned his son, "Don't be so friendly with the chameleon. He might bring us trouble." But the son refused to listen. Fearing that the chameleon might harm them, the Bodhisattva prepared a secret route to escape in case of danger. Meanwhile, the chameleon grew tired of the iguana's friendship and showed a trapper the nesting ground of the iguanas. The trapper lit a fire around it killing most of the iguanas while they tried to escape. But the Bodhisattva and his family ran away unhurt through the secret route. Once they were in a safe place far away from home, the young iguana sought his father's forgiveness and promised never to disobey him.

23 The Rustic Woman

One hot summer afternoon, the king of Benaras was sitting by the window when his eyes fell on a shabbily dressed woman standing on the roadside with an umbrella in her hand. After a while an old beggar came panting for want of breath and collapsed near the woman. The woman at once fetched water from a nearby well and sprinkled the old beggar's face. When the poor man came to his senses, she offered him water to drink while holding her umbrella over his head. Soon the old beggar was back on his feet. The woman gave away her umbrella to the old beggar who accepted it gladly. Seeing such generosity, the king summoned the woman and said, "My lady, you are indeed a noble soul. You may not have riches but you have a kind heart. I'm impressed with what you have done for the poor beggar." Saying so, the king made her his chief queen.

24 King Goodness the Great

The Bodhisattva was once the king of Benaras. He believed only in charity and goodness and was dead against war. He even refused to punish or kill anyone, however guilty they may be. He came to be known as King Goodness the Great. Considering him to be weak, the king of Khosla attacked him. In spite of having a huge army, King Goodness refused to fight back his enemies and instead offered his throne to the enemy king. The king of Khosla was merciless and burying King Goodness and his ministers uptill their necks, left them in the cemetery to be eaten by jackals. Mustering all his strength, King Goodness managed to free himself and his ministers from the jackals. There he came across two demons whom he helped to share their meal equally without fighting and they in turn helped him to get into his palace bedroom with their magical powers. The king of Khosla realised the greatness of king Goodness and returned him his kingdom.

25 New Homes for Tree Spirits

The king of tree spirits once issued a proclamation that each spirit would have to choose a tree to live in and that tree should be happy with its resident spirit. So, all the tree spirits prepared to shift to new homes. There was an old wise tree spirit who advised his fellows to build homes in the forest trees and not on the trees on the outskirts. Most of the tree spirits followed his advice and stayed in the huge old trees in the forest near to the wise old spirit. But there were a few proud ones who said, "We'll go and settle in the trees standing in the villages instead of staying in a crowd. We'll be taken good care of by the villagers." So, a few of them shifted to the tall trees in the villages. One day a terrible storm uprooted most of the trees outside the forest making their resident spirits homeless. But the forest trees together braved the fierce storm and stood safe.

26 The Young Quail

The Bodhisattva was once born as a young quail who lived with his family in a well-protected grass nest. Every morning his parents would go out to fetch food leaving him behind with his brothers. They returned with eatables like figs, worms, grass seeds and the like. His brothers ate whatever their parents brought but the Bodhisattva refused to eat anything except the grass seeds and figs, for he was averse to destroying any form of life, even worms. Consequently his brothers developed strong wings and grew up to be healthy adult quails while the Bodhisattva remained frail and was too weak to fly. Yet he remained happy thinking he had not killed any creature to satisfy his hunger.

27 Champeyya, the Serpent King

The Bodhisattva was once born as Champeyya, the serpent king. He married a beautiful serpent princess called Sumana and led a happy life. However, he soon grew tired of his life of luxury and went to the forest to meditate leaving his wife behind. One day, while he was sitting on an anthill deep in meditation, a snake charmer saw him and trapped him with the help of his magical powers. The serpent king was then made to dance on the streets to the tunes of the snake charmer's flute. Meanwhile his wife went from town to town looking for her husband and at last saw him dancing in the royal court of Benaras. Champeyya stopped his dance at the sight of his tearful wife. Sumana freed her husband with the help of the king and took him home.

28 Baby Peacock

Once the Bodhisattva was born as a peacock. While his mother went out to look for food, she warned him to stay indoors. But the But the baby peacock ignored his mother's advice and went out with his friends to play. As he was enjoying with his friends, some hunters sneaked up on them and caught them one by one. The baby peacock realised his mistake but it was too late. He cried his heart out and thought about his mother, but there was no way of escape. If only the baby peacock had listened to his mother and stayed indoors, he would have been safe.

29 The Legend of the Sparrows

The Bodhisattva was born as a very kind-hearted woman who was always sick. The doctor advised her to feed on the brains of a hundred sparrows after they were being fed with rice and certain herbs for twenty-one days. Her husband brought hundred fat sparrows from the market and putting them in a cage, went to get the herbs from the chemist. The kind woman heard the twittering of the birds in the cage and felt sorry for them. She slowly went near the cage and released all the sparrows. Soon the lady recovered on her own and gave birth to a healthy boy.

30 Self-control

A king had many horses of good breed who helped him win many battles. After one such victory, the king ordered his royal horses to be fed with grape juice. The horses enjoyed the juice and neighed softly to express their gratitude to the king. The donkeys were then fed wih the left over juice after which they brayed loudly. Seeing the king irritated, the chief groom chased the donkeys away saying, "These foolish donkeys lack the decency of the majestic horses."

Contents

The Story of the Month

Magha Regains Compassion

01 Magha Regains Compassion

Once upon a time, during the reign of King Magadha there was a wise man named Magha. He lived in a remote village of thirty families with his four wives Do-gooder, Beauty, Happy and Wellborn. He always followed the path of virtue and thus when he died, he became Sakka, the king of the second lowest heaven. In due course all other people of the village died and since they had always followed the wise teachings of Magha, were all made gods under Sakka. Three of Magha's wives, Do-gooder, Beauty and Happy were very wise and virtuous. So they too turned gods after death and started living with Sakka in the second lowest heaven. So the place was named as "Heaven of Thirty-three". However, The second lowest heaven had been the home of some demons for a long time. Seeing these ugly creatures, Sakka said to his followers, "Why are these demons staying here? This is our place and only we are supposed to live here." Sakka, in his previous birth as Magha, had been kind and just. But now, staying in the comforts of heaven, he had forgotten all his virtues. He didn't want the demons to stay in heaven and planned to get rid of them. He threw a

liquor party in his palace and invited all the demons. They were delighted to be invited and came to the party, cheering loudly. They drank the liquor served by Sakka and his men. After getting them drunk, Sakka drove them out to the lower world. After some time when the demons woke from their stupor they realised that Sakka had thrown them out of their homeland. Enraged, the demons took up arms against Sakka and after a prolonged and fierce battle they emerged victorious. Sakka was thus forced to retreat. While driving past a dense forest, Sakka's chariot ran over a fawn. The mother deer came running to her baby's rescue but it was too late. The fawn had breathed his last. The incident made Sakka realise that life was but transient. Hearing the mother's piteous cries, Sakka regained his earlier good sense

and humanity. His heart was filled with remorse at what he had done to the demons. He said to himself, "I'll never ever take anyone's life for the sake of the heavenly kingdom which is sure to get destroyed some day. I deserve to suffer for what I did. I'll offer my life to the demons and accept whatever punishment they give me." Sakka then ordered his charioteer to take him back to the Heaven of Thirty-three. He went up to the demons and offered to return their kingdom. Seeing Sakka's humble behaviour, the demon king was moved and left along with the other demons to the lower world, leaving the entire heaven for Sakka and the other gods.

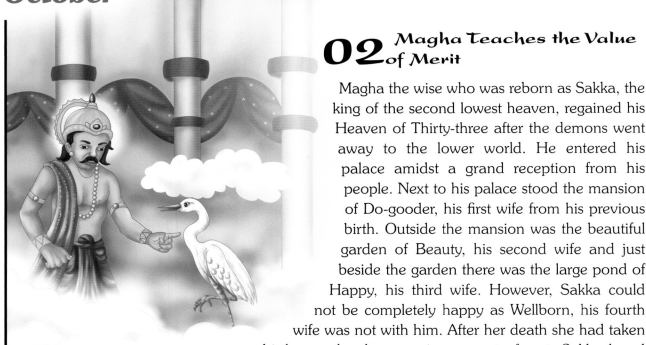

02 Magha Teaches the Value of Merit

Magha the wise who was reborn as Sakka, the king of the second lowest heaven, regained his Heaven of Thirty-three after the demons went away to the lower world. He entered his palace amidst a grand reception from his people. Next to his palace stood the mansion of Do-gooder, his first wife from his previous birth. Outside the mansion was the beautiful garden of Beauty, his second wife and just beside the garden there was the large pond of Happy, his third wife. However, Sakka could not be completely happy as Wellborn, his fourth wife was not with him. After her death she had taken birth as a lovely crane in a remote forest. Sakka loved her dearly and always missed her. One day, Sakka found her and brought her to his kingdom in the Heaven of Thirty-three. He took her to his other wives and said, "Look at your sisters. By doing acts of merit they have earned their place in heaven. And they have gained the utmost happiness in both their lives."

03 The Crane Proves Her Virtue

It was time for the lovely crane to go back to her forest and Sakka said to her, "My dear, in your previous birth as Wellborn, you didn't earn any merit with good work and so you had to be born as a crane. I advice you to atone for your past mistakes and follow the path of virtue." The crane agreed and flew back to her forest. After a few months Sakka wished to see whether the crane was following his advice. So he took the form of a fish and joined a shoal in a river, which flowed by the forest where the crane lived. When he saw her at the riverside, he stealthily swam up and lay motionless in front of her. The crane picked him up thinking he was dead. She was just about to eat him when the fish wiggled his tail slightly. Realising the fish was alive the crane released him into the river. Sakka was very happy to see that the crane had listened to his advice and refrained from killing any more creatures.

04 The Reward for Good Deeds

Sakka assumed his own form and emerged from the water. He blessed the crane and said, "My dear, I am pleased to see your kindness. I assure you that one day you will get rewarded and will be granted an honourable life." Saying this, he returned to Heaven. Eventually the crane died and as a reward for her past good deeds, she took birth as the daughter of a potter in Benaras. After a few years, Sakka again wished to see how his erstwhile wife was doing. He found her in the potter's house and noting that she still followed the path of virtue, felt happy and wished to help her. So he took the guise of an old man and came to her to sell cucumbers. And lo! As soon as she took the cucumbers inside her home, they turned into gold. The girl looked for the old man but he was nowhere to be seen. Soon, the girl and her family became very rich.

05 Well-born Unites with Magha

The potter girl, who in one of her previous births was known as Wellborn, became rich with Sakka's help but remained virtuous. After her death, she was reborn as the daughter of the king of asuras. Gradually, she grew up to be a lovely maiden and when she came of age, her father invited all the asuras to come to his palace where his beautiful daughter would choose her husband. Sakka heard this arrangement and decided to join the asuras disguised as one of them. Sakka sat in the court as the ugliest of the asuras as the princess went round trying to decide who would be the right husband for her. Perhaps because of her past relationship with him, the girl felt a strong attraction for Sakka and chose him as her husband. At last, Sakka was united with Wellborn and they lived happily ever after.

October

06 A Questioning Mind

The chief advisor of King Brahmadatta was a highly knowledgeable man who came from a family known for its wealth and high lineage. He was also a very generous man and was highly respected by all. One day he thought, "The king respects me the most. Is it because of my knowledge, my noble birth and wealth or my goodness?" He planned to find the truth with the help of an experiment. He went to the royal coin maker and pretended to take great interest in how gold coins were made. Then, while watching, he picked up one gold coin in full view of the coin maker and walked away. As he had thought the coin maker saw everything but didn't utter a word considering the good reputation of the priest.

07 How the Priest Loses His Reputation

The priest again went to the coin maker on the following day and this time he picked up two gold coins. The coin maker noticed everything but again did nothing to stop him. Finally on the third day, the priest took a handful of coins, but this time the coin maker could not hold himself back. He caught hold of the priest's hands and shouted, "You thief! I have been noticing you for the past few days. What fools we were to think you were an honorable man!" His words drew the attention of others and when they learnt about the matter they beat up the priest in fury, tied his hands behind his back and dragged him to the king. "Shame on you! You were an example of goodness to all of us. And now to think that all your goodness was actually pretension..." they yelled at the priest. Their words proved to the priest that the people respected him for his goodness.

08 The Priest Finds His Answer

As the people took the priest to the king, they came upon a few snake charmers who were entertaining onlookers with some snakes, including a poisonous cobra. The snakes danced and wrapped around their necks as the charmers played the flute. The priest was taken aback by their daring acts and warned the snake charmers not to play with the snakes, especially the cobra. But the snake charmers ignored him saying, "We know the real nature of the snake. It's more important to be careful about people like you who put up a sweet face but are poisonous inside." Hearing this, the priest realised that goodness is the quality that people admire most in this world." In the court, he explained all his actions to the king. The king released him and the priest again resumed his honorable position in the court.

09 King Kalabu and Kundaka Kumar

Once upon a time, during the reign of King Kalabu, the Bodhisattva was born as Kundaka Kumar, the son of a wealthy merchant. After his parents' death the Bodhisattva renounced his family life and went to the Himalayas to live there as an ascetic. After a while he again came back to Varanasi, which was once his home. The army commander of Varanasi invited the holy sage to the palace. But since the Bodhisattva was averse to staying in anybody's house, he decided to stay in the royal park. One day, King Kalabu came to the park along with his queens. After hours of making merry, the king became tired and gradually drifted off. Seeing the king asleep, the queens went roaming in the garden and came across the Bodhisattva. The queens paid their respect to him and requested him to give them some religious discourses. Meanwhile, the king woke up and was surprised to see himself alone. Not finding his queens anywhere, he ordered his sentries to look for them.

10 Kundaka Kumar Teaches Forbearance

The sentries of King Kalabu reported to the king that his queens were in the company of an ascetic. Hearing this, the king flew into a terrible rage and rushed to the scene. As he drew his sword to kill the Bodhisattva, the queens pleaded for mercy and asked him to spare the ascetic's life. Still seething, the king asked, "Holy man! What do you teach? "The value of forbearance. I teach others how one can never lose composure even in the face of abuse," answered the Bodhisattva calmly. "Aha! Is that so?" the king sniggered. "Then let me test your forbearance." Saying this, he ordered his men to lash the ascetic hundred times with a whip of thorns. The thorns bruised his back sorely but still the Bodhisattva remained calm. This infuriated the king all the more and he chopped off the Bodhisattva's hands and legs. "Now holy man, tell me what you teach," the king demanded. But this time too, the Bodhisattva smiled and replied, "The value of forbearance." The king became frustrated and left the scene. On his way, he was struck by lightning and died.

11 Wise Birds and Foolish Birds

Once there lived a flock of birds on a giant tree in a forest. One day, the leader of the birds noticed two branches rubbing against each other causing wood to fall in powder. Then, taking a closer look, the leader saw that tiny wisps of smoke were coming out due to the friction. The bird realised that a fire was starting and immediately called for a meeting. He addressed his fellow birds and said, "My friends, this tree has started to catch fire. Before this fire burns everything, I think it will be wise for us to leave the forest." The wise birds agreed and flew away to find a new home for themselves. But there were some foolish ones who were reluctant to leave the cozy comfort of their homes. "The leader is always so panicky. He makes mountains out of molehills. There is no danger," they said and stayed back. And in a short while, raging flames engulfed the whole forest and these foolish birds were burned to death.

12 The Tortoise's Home

Once upon a time there was a big lake linked to the river Ganga, where lived many fish and tortoises. One day, knowing by instinct that the following year would be dry, they all swam into the river for safety. One tortoise, however, stayed behind. "This lake has always been my home. My parents, too, have lived and died here. I have so many memories surrounding this place. I can't leave it for a new home," thought he and stayed back. Then in the summer when the water dried up, he dug a hole in the bed of the lake and stayed buried. One day a potter came to collect some clay and with a spade dug the bed where the tortoise was lying hidden. The spade hit the tortoise hard, causing his death. Thus the creature met his end for clinging to his memories and not acting according to the need of the hour.

13 The Royal Barber

Once in the city of Vesali there lived a royal barber who was a devoted follower of Buddha. One day, he went to the palace for work taking his son along. There his son got attracted to a very beautiful girl all dressed up like a goddess and wanted to marry her. His father told him to forget about the girl as she belonged to the royal family and would never agree to such a proposal. But the son refused to eat and drink until he got married to her. All his family members tried to reason with him, but failed. The young lover was so disappointed and heartbroken that he passed away. After performing his son's last rites, the father went to meet Buddha. Buddha told him "Your son has died by setting his heart on something which he could never have" The barber could say nothing but weep for his son's foolishness.

October

14 The Golden Goose and the Palasa Tree

Once upon a time the Bodhisattva was born as a golden goose. Every day he flew around in search of food and on his way would perch on a palasa tree to take rest. Gradually, a strong bond developed between him and the tree spirit that lived on the palasa. One day a bird dropped a seed of a banyan tree in a crack of the palasa tree and a sapling sprang from it. The Bodhisattva noticed it and knew it could be dangerous for his friend. He immediately drew his friend's attention to it and said, "My dear friend, destroy this sapling right now before it grows up and destroys you." But the tree spirit brushed aside his warning saying, "What can a sapling do to me, my friend? You don't have to worry." The sapling soon grew up till it became so strong and heavy that it crushed the palasa tree. Thus the tree spirit met his end due to his overconfidence.

15 The Carpenter's Boar

Once, a carpenter found a little boar in a pit, who was almost dying. He took him home and reared him calling him Tacchasukara. When he grew up and was strong enough to protect himself, the carpenter set him free. Tacchasukara joined his fellow boars in the jungle. At that time a tiger was preying on the boars and had killed a good number of them. Tacchasukara planned a strategy and succeeded in killing the tiger. The other boars were very pleased to get a strong and an intelligent friend and told him that a man who posed as an ascetic had actually helped the tiger kill the boars. Learning this, Tacchasukara charged at the pretender with his mates. Seeing the approaching boars, the man ran for his life and climbed up a fig tree. But the boars uprooted the tree and killed the man. Then they declared Tacchasukara their king, making him sit on the fig tree and sprinkling him with water from the conch shell, which the ascetic used for drinking water. Since then it became a custom to coronate a king by seating him on fig wood and sprinkling him with water from a conch shell.

182

16 The King of the World

The Bodhisattva was born as Clear-sighted, a wise ruler of a prosperous kingdom called Kusavati. He set down ten rules which he strictly followed in ruling his kingdom—uprooting ill will, defeating open enmity, protecting innocence, promoting self-control, patience, gentleness, charity, generosity, straightforwardness and goodness. The people were all happy to have him as a ruler.

Kings from far and wide requested him to guide them in matters of administration. In due course his rule was embraced by one and all and he became the king of the world. His reputation spread far and wide and people considered him immortal. They now called him Clear-sighted the Great. Years passed and one day Clear-sighted breathed his last saying that whosoever is born is sure to die irrespective of his rank or position. And thus the king of the world too left for his heavenly abode after leading a glorious life.

17 Don't Loose Your Faith

Once there was a group of merchants who were crossing a vast desert. Having travelled for a long time, they were very tired and thirsty but could not find a drop of water to drink anywhere in the vast sandy wastes.

Fearing they might all be dead before they reached their destination, they began digging a well in the sand with the hope of finding water underneath. They kept on digging and still they could not find a single drop. Tired, they sat down to cry helplessly. There was a little boy in the group who, unlike the other merchants, had great determination and continued digging deeper without stopping. Suddenly, a jet of water gushed out and everyone was overjoyed to see it. At the same time, they also felt ashamed of themselves for loosing their faith so easily and learnt a lesson from a little boy.

18 Ananda's Gift

Once there lived a monk named Ananda who used to preach the holy sermons of the Bodhisattva to the ladies of the royal household. Pleased with his teachings, the ladies gifted him with five hundred new garments. The king met Ananda and gave him another five hundred garments. Ananda gifted all the garments to a young monk who had always helped him in times of need. This monk in turn donated the garments to the other monks in the monastery. These monks, however, felt annoyed that Ananda had favoured only one young monk with so many gifts and brought up the matter with the Bodhisattva. "Ananda has tried to repay the many favours this monk had done him," said the Bodhisattva with a smile. This made the monks feel ashamed of their jealousy and they sought Ananda's forgiveness, promising never to draw conclusions without knowing the truth.

19 The Thankless Monkey

A kind gentleman lived near a grove of banyan trees. Under a banyan tree was a well where the passersby stopped to quench their thirst. A group of monkeys lived on the banyan trees and, in order to help them drink water, the man placed a trough by the side of the well so that whoever drank water from the well used to fill the trough with water for the monkeys. One hot summer day, a thirsty monkey came to drink water but as no one had passed by, the trough was empty. Seeing him, the kind man filled the trough. The monkey quenched his thirst and then started making faces at the man. Annoyed, the man asked, "Is this how you return my favour?" At this the monkey gave a loud screech and climbing up the tree, spat on the man. The man scowled in anger and decided never to pour any water in the trough again.

20 Silence Is Golden

Once there was a dark-skinned Brahmin who was the king's chaplain. He was jealous of the prosperity of another dark-skinned Brahmin. He advised the king to rebuild the southern gates of the city and sacrifice a dark-skinned Brahmin as part of the inaugural ceremony. The king agreed to do as advised. Meanwhile, the chaplain spoke about the plan to the king's wife and soon the whole city came to know about it. As a result, all the dark-skinned Brahmins fled from the city leaving behind only the chaplain. On the auspicious day when no other dark-skinned Brahmin could be found, the king, on the people's request, decided to sacrifice the

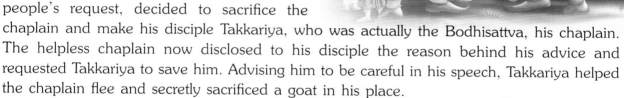

chaplain and make his disciple Takkariya, who was actually the Bodhisattva, his chaplain. The helpless chaplain now disclosed to his disciple the reason behind his advice and requested Takkariya to save him. Advising him to be careful in his speech, Takkariya helped the chaplain flee and secretly sacrificed a goat in his place.

21 The Monk's Dilemma

The Bodhisattva was once an ascetic residing in the royal park of Pancala. The king treated him with great honour and respect. Twelve years passed by and it was time for the ascetic to return his home in the Himalayas. He went up to the king and said, "O benevolent ruler, you have been a kind host to me and I have enjoyed my stay in your royal park. But now I need to go back to my hermitage." The king sadly agreed to let him go and decided to give him a farewell gift. The ascetic had always wanted a pair of single-soled shoes and a leaf umbrella but had always hesitated to ask the king thinking that it would make him weep to have to ask or to be refused. But the king knew his feelings and offered him all he had. The ascetic just took what he needed—a pair of shoes and a leaf umbrella and left.

22 King Sibi

God once sent two of his messengers in the form of a falcon and a dove to the court of King Sibi to test his devotion and compassion. The falcon started chasing the dove as if to catch him. The king asked the falcon to have mercy and spare the bird. The falcon refused saying he was hungry. The king offered him the best of food, but the falcon said, "I can feed on nothing but flesh of animals." The king then cut a part of his flesh equal to the weight of the dove and offered it to the falcon but it turned out to be lighter than the body of the dove. Every time the king cut a portion of his flesh and weighed it against the dove, the latter turned out to be heavier. At last King Sibi offered the whole of his body in exchange of the dove. At this, God appeared before him and said, "You have indeed shown compassion for the dove and is worthy to be called the Bodhisattva or the Enlightened One." From then on King Sibi became the Bodhisattva.

23 Jotipala, the great sage

The Bodhisattva was once born as Jotipala, the son of a priest. He grew up to be a skilful archer and was recruited by the king for a salary of a thousand rupees a day. This made the other servants of the king jealous and they started hating Jotipala for his success. Their behaviour greatly disturbed Jotipala and he often wondered, "Why do people hate each other?" In due course, the king made Jotipala the chief archer. But before accepting his new post Jotipala came to the realisation that all evil is caused by worldly attachments and decided to go into deep meditation in the forest. Thus at midnight he dressed in plain saffron robes and left his house in search of truth. He built a hut in the midst of a dense forest and started living the life of an ascetic. Soon many people including his parents and the king joined him as followers and thus Jotipala became a famous sage.

24 Noble Sankicca

Once, the Bodhisattva was born as Sankicca in the family of the chaplain of the king of Benaras. Since early childhood the prince of Benaras and Sankicca were close friends. The prince grew up to be power hungry and planned to grab the throne by murdering his father. When Sankicca came to know about it he tried hard to dissuade him but all his efforts went in vain. Broken-hearted, Sankicca left Benaras and started leading the life of an ascetic in the Himalayas. After some time the prince was filled with remorse and longed for his lost friend. But it was not until fifty years later that Sankicca visited Benaras again and met the king who had lost his peace of mind and was leading a restless life. Sankicca told him many harrowing tales of the hell where sinners had to suffer after death. He then went on to narrate tales of the beautiful world of the devas where the purified souls attain ultimate happiness. These words of wisdom at last gave the king a sense of peace.

25 Tayodhamma, the monkey king

Once there lived a monkey king named Tayodhamma. A jealous ruler, Tayodhamma feared even the strength of his newborn sons and killed them soon after they were born. So the monkey queen went to a distant land and delivered a monkey prince, who was actually the Bodhisattva. When the prince grew up, he came to meet his father. Seeing his young son before him, Tayodhamma at once decided to kill him, lest his son should overthrow him. Pretending to embrace him, Tayodhamma tried to break his bones, but failed. So he sent him to collect lotus flowers from a pond which he knew was guarded by a demon saying, "Son, I shall crown you with my own hands once you get me the flowers." But the prince knew about the demon and so he very carefully plucked the flowers swinging low from a creeper without touching the water. The demon was pleased to see such wisdom and became the prince's disciple. When the king saw his son approaching with the ferocious demon, he died out of fear.

26 The Selfish Fisherman

In a fishing village, lived a fisherman who was very selfish. One day, as the fisherman spread his net in the river, his line was pulled by a snag. Thinking it to be a big fish, the fisherman decided to have the entire fish for himself without sharing with his neighbours. So he called his son and said, "Listen, I think I have caught a very big fish. But we need to keep it a secret, else we will have to share it with all our neighbours and won't have more for ourselves. So go home and tell your mother to pick up a quarrel with the neighbours on some pretext."

The son ran home and informed his mother. The fisherman's wife, who too was selfish woman appreciated her husband's plan and started calling names to her neighbours. Unable to understand what the matter was, the neighbours came to ask her and the sly woman started abusing them. So a quarrel broke out and the neighbours took her to the village chief where she was badly beaten up for having picked up a quarrel with the neighbours for no reason. Meanwhile, the fisherman went into the water to drag out the fish. But alas! He struck against the snag and became blind. The blind fisherman cried for help but none came to his aid. Thus, the fisherman had to pay a heavy price for his selfishness.

27 God's Punishment

The king of Benaras once held a festival, which was attended by gods and humans. The gods wore wreaths of flowers, the sweet fragrance of which filled the air. Everyone was charmed and asked for a wreath to wear. "These can only be worn by people possessing certain virtues," said the gods. The king's chaplain, a clever Brahmin, declared that he possessed those virtues. The floral wreath was placed on his head and the gods disappeared. The moment the chaplain wore the wreath, he was seized with unbearable headache. He tried to put it away but the wreath would not come off. For seven days the chaplain suffered extreme pain till at last the king took pity on him and held another similar festival. There the chaplain confessed his guilt and was relieved from the pain.

28 The Story of the Two Brothers

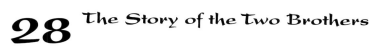

The Bodhisattva was once born as the son of a rich Brahmin. He was named Sona and had a younger brother named Nanda. Both the boys were well-educated and possessed magical powers. When they grew up, their parents asked them to get married and settle down. But the two brothers refused and expressed their desire to become ascetics. At this, the parents also decided to follow their sons and the entire family became ascetics. One day, when Nanda brought unripe fruits for his parents, Sona lost his temper and banished him from sight. Nanda left the forest feeling sad. He joined the king and with his magical powers, helped him to defeat his enemies who in turn helped Nanda win his brother's forgiveness and reunite with his family once again.

29 The Deceitful Crow

A crow once visited the island of birds and longed to feast on the birds' fledglings and eggs. He stood on one leg with his mouth open and declared that he was a holy being who lived on nothing else but wind. Believing the sly crow, the birds requested him to watch over their eggs and babies while they went to gather food. When the birds were gone, the crow went up to their nests and ate up most of the eggs and babies. When the birds returned, they raised a hue and cry looking for their young ones and eggs without for once suspecting the crow who they believed was a holy being. Days passed and one day the Bodhisattva, who was the king of the birds, secretly kept watch, caught the crow red-handed and punished him.

30 The Devoted Son

The Bodhisattva was once born as a very pious boy named Saput. He was a very devoted son and took good care of his old parents. Now Saput's parents had aged and all their teeth had fallen off. So it was very difficult for them to chew their food. Unable to have proper meals, his parents became weak day by day. Saput felt very sorry for his parents and decided to do something for them. "All my parents can have is milk. I should do something to get the mountain deer's milk," thought Saput. So he decided to dress like a baby deer and put on a deer's head and go to the mountain everyday so that the deer would mistake him to be one among them and allow him to mingle with them. Every morning Saput left for the mountain disguising himself like a baby deer and grazed with them. Thinking him to be a baby, the she-mountain deer allowed Saput to have her milk. Saput kept storing the milk in the little pots that he hid under his garment. In the evening, he used to take the deer's milk to his house and feed his parents. Soon his parents regained their health and Saput lived happily with them.

31 Truth can Never Be Hidden

The Bodhisattva was once born as the God of birds, Garuda. He changed his form to a handsome young man and often played dice with the king of Benaras who had a beautiful queen called Sussondi. Once, while playing dice, Garuda saw Sussondi and fell for her beauty. "I need to have this beautiful lady as my wife," thought Garuda and decided to marry her. With his supernatural powers, Garuda raised a storm in the city and covered it with dark clouds. Under the cover of darkness, he carried Sussondi with him. The king was full of grief for his queen and called his most trusted minister Sagga, unaware that his friend Garuda had carried away his wife. "O, wise friend. Please help me find my beloved queen. Search in every nook and corner and bring her back to me," the king requested Sagga. So Sagga along with a few soldiers went looking for the queen. Meanwhile, Garuda kept coming to play dice with the king so he was never suspected. Sailing for days together, Sagga at last came to the island where Garuda had kept Sassondi. Garuda was away playing dice and Sassondi took advantage of his absence. He secretly climbed into the queen's chamber and called out, "Your Highness, the king is heart broken without you. His majesty has sent me to take you back to him safely." He then carried back the queen to the king. The king embraced his queen with tears of joy and seeing their love, Garuda realised his mistake.

Contents

The Story of the Month

The Prince and the She-devil

01 The Prince and the She-devil

Once, the Bodhisattva was born as the son of King Brahmadatta of Benaras. He was the youngest of the hundred sons the king had. As he grew up he became the strongest and wisest of all his brothers. But since he was the youngest prince he had no hope of becoming the king. One day, he asked the Silent Buddhas whether he stood any chance of being crowned. The Silent Buddhas informed him that if he could reach Takkasila within seven days, he might become the king of Takkasila. But they also informed him about the dangerous "Devil Wood" that would fall on his way. Next morning, the prince along with his five servants set off for Takkasila. He carried a charmed string and some sand, which would ward off evil forces. However, while crossing Devil Wood he lost all his five servants who, inspite of his warnings succumbed to temptations laid down by the devils. Alone, he continued on his journey to Takkasila. A she-devil, particularly keen on catching the prince, said, "A-ha! This young prince seems to enjoy total control over his five senses. But I'll not rest until I eat his soft flesh." Saying this, the devil followed the prince taking the form of a beautiful woman. She tried hard to attract his attention, but such was his self-control that the prince didn't even look at her for once. After reaching Takkasila, the Bodhisattva went straight into a rest house. Since he carried the charmed string and the sand the devil could not follow him inside. Just then, the king of Takkasila was passing by on his royal chariot taking his regular round around the city. He was so charmed to see the beautiful woman on the roadside that he instantly fell in love with her. He got down from his chariot and asked her, "Why are you standing here, dear lady?" "My husband is inside the rest house and he is refusing to accept me as his wife," answered the devil sorrowfully. Hearing this, the Bodhisattva came out and said, "She is no wife of mine. She is a devil and she intends to eat me." At this the devil broke into false tears. Sobbing pitiably she cried, "O lord! What shall I do if my husband leaves me?" The king felt very sorry for her, took her into his palace and married her that very day. Now, as the devil was away from the Devil Wood, she had lost her power to subdue others unless they themselves succumbed to temptation. So at night in the royal bedchamber, the devil told the king, "O my lord, I am sure everyone here envies my good fortune. Give me such power that none can harm me." Hearing this, the king gave her his arm band and said, "Wear this band. No one within the palace can ever harm you." At night when all fell asleep, the devil killed and ate everyone within the palace compound. Even animals were not spared. Next morning people discovered the remains of the dead. They realised that what the Bodhisattva had said about the woman was true. His wisdom and self-control impressed them and he was made the new king of Takkasila.

02 A Man Named Bad

Once, in Takkasila, there was a student called Bad who studied under a renowned teacher. The student was not happy with his name. He felt that since his name was Bad, everyone took him to be so. So one day he went up to his teacher and said, "Sir, I don't like to be called Bad. Please suggest a nicer name for me." The teacher asked him to search himself for a better name. The student travelled for many days across cities and came across many names, but liked none. He then came to a big city where he saw a funeral procession passing. He asked a passerby the name of the dead man. "His name was Alive," replied the man. "Alive is now dead!" cried the startled student. "So what if his name was Alive? Does your name matter at all? Under any name, be it Dead or Alive, a person is sure to die. Even a fool knows that," said the man.

03 Bad Learns to Accept His Name

The student whose name was Bad now felt a bit comfortable about his name knowing that a man named Alive could be dead. He continued on his way across the city and saw a man being beaten up by some people. "This man was supposed to repay me today. But he has failed to do so," said one among them when Bad inquired the reason. Bad then asked his name. "His name is Rich," informed another man. "Rich!" exclaimed Bad. "A man named Rich is in debt!" "So what if his name is Rich? Your name has nothing to do with your financial condition," said the creditor. After hearing this, Bad became even more disinterested in changing his name. Then he met a man who had lost his way. He came to know that the man's name was Tour-guide. "Tour-guide has lost his way!" said he visibly amused. "It does not matter whether my name is Tour-guide or Tourist. A name is just a word to recognise a person." Hearing this, Bad realised that a name never signifies the character and the condition of a person. So he dropped the idea of changing his name.

04 The Wealthy Prince

The Bodhisattva was once born into a wealthy family and led a life of comfort. But unlike others, he liked to spend most of his time in meditation and disliked the luxuries of life. After his parents died, he became an ascetic and went to the forest to meditate. Soon his selflessness, modesty and politeness won the hearts of the villagers. One day, a friend of his father's came to meet him and tried to persuade him to return home saying he had neglected his duties as a son, brother, husband and father. But the Bodhisattva was adamant and said, "It's easy to lead a worldly life as a common man. But to get rid of all comforts and live for others is difficult." His father's friend saw the crowd, which had gathered to listen to the Bodhisattva's discourse and realised that his friend's son had indeed achieved what no common man ever could and went back.

05 The Naïve Householder

Once upon a time, there lived a gentle householder in a village not far from Kashi. One day, a devastating flood washed away all the crops, leaving the villagers in deep trouble. So the householder went to the headman of the village to ask for help. The wicked headman gave them an ox to plough the fields against an agreement that the villagers repaid him within two months after the harvest. He knew fully well that it would be impossible for them to do so. He longed to possess whatever little the villagers had. However, this headman happened to be a close friend of the wife of one of the householder. The householder had time and again scolded his wife for being friends with the headman. The wife too had promised to break off the relationship but secretly maintained contact with him. The householder suspected the truth and planning to catch the two red-handed, he pretended to go abroad.

06 The Naive Householder Teaches the Headman a Lesson

As soon as the gentle householder left his home, the wicked headman came over. Together with the woman, he sat planning various ways of cheating the villagers when suddenly the householder appeared at the door. Seeing him, they quickly planned to save the situation and started acting accordingly. When the householder entered, he found the headman shouting at the woman, "I don't want to listen to anything. Ask your husband to pay for the ox or return it right away." The woman, who was standing in front of the granary as if to guard it from the headman, retorted back, "What can my husband do? We have nothing in the granary. How can you expect us to pay you so soon?" But their playacting could not deceive the wise householder. He knew it was not yet time to repay the headman nor was there any grain in the granary for the woman to guard. In a fit of rage, the householder hit the headman so hard that he fainted. Then he threw his wife out of his house.

07 The Story of the Elephant King Goodness

Once upon a time, there lived a magnificent white elephant in a deep jungle not far from Benaras. His gentleness and wisdom endeared him to all the elephants of the jungle and they unanimously declared him their king. He came to be known as King Goodness. King Goodness loved his subjects dearly but never felt comfortable with all the admiration. So to live by himself, he went to stay in the quieter side of the forest. One day a forester from Benaras came to the jungle in search of things he could take back to the city. While roaming around, he lost his way and ran here and there with no success. In utter distress and exhaustion, he broke down and started wailing, imploring the gods to save him. His pitiable cries reached the ears of the generous elephant and he came to help the man out of his trouble.

08 Elephant King Goodness Saves a Forester

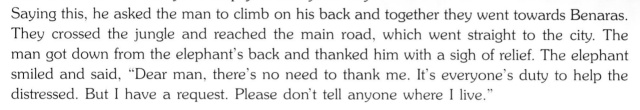

The forester was at first frightened at the sight of an elephant coming towards him. But King Goodness asked politely, "My dear friend, what has happened to you? Why are you wandering in the forest?" "O dear elephant, I have lost my way. I don't know how to get back to Benaras," said the forester helplessly. The elephant smiled and replied, "Dear friend, there's no need to worry. I'll help you find your way."

Saying this, he asked the man to climb on his back and together they went towards Benaras. They crossed the jungle and reached the main road, which went straight to the city. The man got down from the elephant's back and thanked him with a sigh of relief. The elephant smiled and said, "Dear man, there's no need to thank me. It's everyone's duty to help the distressed. But I have a request. Please don't tell anyone where I live."

09 The Forester Deceives Elephant King Goodness

The forester was an ungrateful person. He met some ivory carvers in the market in Benaras and asked them, "Would you like to have the tusks of a living elephant?" "Tusks from a living elephant!" exclaimed the carvers. "Are you sure you can bring us such tusks? Ivory from a living elephant, is more precious than that of a dead one. If you can bring it we'll give you any price you want." The forester's eyes gleamed in greed. Forgetting all the help he got from the elephant he went back to King Goodness. "O great elephant. I am going through very bad times. I have turned a pauper and have many debts to clear. Can you give me a small piece of your tusk so that I get some money by selling it?" pleaded he. The elephant was so generous that he immediately offered his tusk. Without any remorse the man cut some big pieces and took them home. He sold the pieces to the ivorycarvers and got a good price.

199

10 The Forester Pays for His Cruelty

The forester became rich by selling the ivory he got from King Goodness. But greed overpowered him and he asked the elephant if he could have the rest of the tusk on the pretext of still being poor. The elephant felt sorry for him and readily agreed. The forester cut off the rest of the tusk and went away. But still he was not satisfied. On another day, he again went to the elephant and said with a harried face, "O dear, when shall good luck smile upon me? I am still leading a hand-to-mouth existence. Can I get the root of your ivory to sell?" The generous elephant agreed at once and the pitiless man dug out the roots of his tusks, leaving the elephant in extreme pain. This sordid act of cruelty shook everything from Heaven to Hell and when the man was returning, the earth beneath his feet split wide open and the burning flames of hell rose up and swallowed him in the abyss.

11 Canda and the King of Benaras

Once upon a time the Bodhisattva was born as a kinnara or celestial musician. During summers, he would come down to the plains on Earth and live with his beloved Canda on the foothills of the Canda Mountain. One day, while they were frolicking in the water of a stream, King Brahmadatta was passing by. His eyes fell on the lovely Canda singing and dancing gaily in the water and he fell in love with her. Guessing that the kinnara was her husband, King Brahmadatta shot and killed him with his arrow. He thought that with the kinnara dead, Canda would agree to marry him. But soon he was proved wrong. Canda sat wailing aloud beside her dead husband, when King Brahmadatta came up and offered his love to her. But Canda flared up at his words. "How could you think that I would forgive the man who has killed my husband?" she shouted. Her heartrending cries shook Sakka's throne in Heaven. Pleased with Canda's devotion, Sakka came down and restored the Bodhisattva's life.

12 Ruhaka and His Foolish Wife

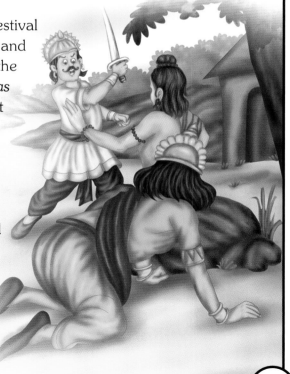

Once the Bodhisattva was born as the king of Benaras. He had a chaplain named Ruhaka whom he gifted a horse of high breed dressed in bejewelled trappings. When Ruhaka rode it on the streets, he drew everyone's attention. "What a majestic horse Ruhaka has got! And look at the rich trappings," they would say, pointing at him. His wife thought that Ruhaka himself would be applauded in the same way if he wore the trappings. At first, Ruhaka laughed at the proposal, saying the trappings of a horse would look strange on him. But the woman went on persisting till Ruhaka agreed. Next day, when he went out putting on the trappings, all the people laughed and jeered at him. Angry with his foolish wife, Ruhaka came home determined to punish her. But the wife had already taken shelter with the king anticipating Ruhaka's temper. The Bodhisattva then pacified his anger saying that he should forgive her as it was the nature of women to commit acts of folly.

13 Love and Kindness

One year, the king of Benaras held a grand festival celebrating his conquest of an enemy kingdom. Kings and emperors from all over the world, attended the festivities. Even the *yakshas*, nagas and the *garudas* took part in the celebrations. It so happened that amidst all the revelry, a naga laid his hand on his neighbour's shoulder without noticing that he was a garuda. Now, *garudas* and nagas were age-old enemies and the former always maintained an upper hand over the other. So when the naga realised his mistake he was frightened and ran for his life pursued by the *garuda*. They ran and ran until the naga hid behind an ascetic meditating beside his hermitage. Out of respect, the *garuda* took care not to hurt the holy man. Knowing their never-ending enmity, the ascetic taught them the value of love and kindness. His soothing words wiped away their hatred and soon they became friends.

14 The Prince and the Brahmin

Once the Bodhisattva was born as Junha, the son of King Brahmadatta of Benaras. One day, while walking down a road in Takkasila where he was sent for studying, he accidentally ran into a poor Brahmin knocking him down and scattering all his alms. Even his begging bowl broke into pieces. Junha was very sorry for the damage and said to the Brahmin. "Sir, I am very sorry to have caused you so much loss. Right now, I don't have any money to help you. But I promise to compensate you handsomely in future when I am the king. Please remind me once I ascend the throne." In due course, Junha became the king of Benaras. One day, while on his daily round around the city, the Brahmin came in front of his chariot and held out his hand crying, "Long live the king!" and asked for the help that he had promised. At first Junha didn't recognise him but when the Brahmin narrated the incident, he remembered instantly and showered him profusely with gifts.

15 Yuvanjaya

Once upon a time the Bodhisattva was born as Yuvanjaya, the eldest son of Sabbadatta, the king of Benaras. Early one morning Yuvanjaya went out on his chariot to see for himself how the people of the kingdom were leading their lives. On his way he saw beautiful dewdrops adorning blades of grass like pearls. The sight was so pleasing that it made a deep impression on his mind. When Yuvanjaya was returning, it was late in the afternoon. He looked for those dewdrops on the grass but found none. Seeing him upset, his charioteer said, "My lord, how can you find dewdrops at this hour of the day? Dew doesn't stay for long. The sun has dried up all the dewdrops you saw at dawn." Hearing this, a sudden realisation came to his mind that everything was like dewdrops, which stayed for some time before time took its toll. He lost interest in worldly things and soon after became an ascetic.

16 The Power of Prayers

Once upon a time the Bodhisattva was a little quail. Although he had tiny wings and feet, he could not walk or fly. He depended entirely on his parents who brought him food and fed him with their beaks. One day, the forest where they lived caught fire. Some birds died and some flew away to save their lives. But the parents of the little quail were reluctant to leave him. The little quail begged and begged them to escape until they agreed. Then the quail, who was known for his virtue, prayed to the gods for the well-being of all the birds who were still trapped in the burning forest. He also prayed for his dear parents and others who managed to save themselves. Then he wished hard for the forest to be safe from fire for the next million of years. His earnest and selfless prayers touched the heart of the gods and the fire stopped.

17 A Man Named Curse

Once there lived a wise man named Anathapindika. He had a friend whose name was Curse while Anathapindika was prosperous, Curse was still an unsuccessful man. Frustrated, Curse approached his friend for a job and Anathapindika put him in charge of his finances. Since then, Curse began to stay in Anathapindika's house. But Anathapindika's friends and relatives were not too happy with Curse's presence as he had an inauspicious name. But Anathapindika didn't pay any heed to their objections. "A name is just a way to recognise a person. One should never be judged by one's name," said he. A few days later Anathapindika went to a distant village with his all his servants. Curse was alone in the house. At night robbers approached the house knowing it was unoccupied. But Curse was alert and when he saw robbers had surrounded the house, he quickly thought out a plan.

18 Curse Saves the House from Robbers

Curse started running about in the house creating a lot of noise as if he was waking up everyone. He started blowing the conch and beating drums so that it would seem the whole house was getting ready to fight the robbers. The robbers were confused and scared. "The house is not as unprotected as we thought. Our informer tipped us all wrong. Anathapindika must be present today," said the leader. "Yes leader, I think we better not make an attempt today. Let's go back," said his deputy. So the robbers dropped their cudgels and ran away. Next morning, when the neighbours saw the cudgels, they guessed what had happened. They praised Curse for his courage and presence of mind. "What an intelligent friend Anathapindika has! Had it not been for him Anathapindika would have lost all his money," they said among themselves.

19 Curse Gains Respect

Anathapindika returned from the village and his friends and neighbours told him how Curse had saved his house from the robbers. Anathapindika rushed to his friend and holding his hands said, "O dear Curse, I always knew you're unlike your name. Last night you proved me right. I am really very lucky to have you as my friend and will remain grateful to you forever." His words soothed Curse's mind, as he had always felt unhappy with his name. He felt happy that he had saved his childhood friend from ruin. Anathapindika then turned towards the others and said, "Many of you who are present here had advised me to throw out my friend because he has an inauspicious name. Had I listened to you, I would have been ruined. I hope after this incident you all realise that a name does not indicate a person's character. I am sure everyone will learn a lesson from this incident and try to get rid of superstitions."

20 Rohanta, the Golden Deer

Once the Bodhisattva was born as a golden deer named Rohanta. He lived with his brother Cittamiga and sister Sutana near a lake. One day, Khema, the queen of Benaras, had a dream that a golden deer was preaching to her. Next morning, she begged her husband to bring her the deer. The king sent hunters all across his kingdom to search for the deer. One hunter who knew Rohanta's whereabouts laid a trap by the side of the river where Rohanta and his fellow deer usually drank water. Rohanta stepped on the trap and got caught. He immediately shouted to warn the other deer so that they could run away and save themselves. Everyone fled except Cittamiga and Sutana. No amount of persuasion could keep them away from Rohanta. Their love for their brother touched the hunter's heart and he released the deer. Rohanta then taught him the value of love and kindness. His teachings changed the hunter's nature and he became an ascetic.

21 The Antelope and His Friends

Once there lived an antelope in a dense wood near a big lake. A woodpecker lived on a nearby tree and in the lake dwelled a tortoise. They were close friends and lived happily together. One day, a hunter saw the antelope's footprints near the lake and laid a trap to catch him. At night when the antelope came down to the lake to drink water, he stepped on the leather noose and got trapped. His desperate cries reached his friends' ears and hurriedly they came to the spot. All three of them put their heads together and thought out a plan. "Dear Tortoise, you bite this leather noose and tear it off. Meanwhile I'll fly to the hunter's house and check what he is doing. I'll try to keep him away from the forest as long as possible," said the woodpecker to the tortoise. Thus the tortoise started gnawing at the leather noose and the woodpecker flew down to the hunter's house.

22 The Woodpecker and the Tortoise Save the Antelope

At the break of dawn, the hunter came out of his house carrying his knife with him. As soon as the woodpecker, who had kept watch all through the night, saw him, he flapped his wings and struck the hunter on his face. The hunter took it as an ill omen and thought it better to stay at home for a while. A little later, he again got up to start for the forest. This time he tried to come out of the back door to avoid any more trouble. But this time too the woodpecker struck him again. "Twice I have been struck by this ominous bird. I think it's not the right time to go out. I'll wait a bit and go after sunrise," thought the hunter. In the meantime, the tortoise had gnawed off the entire noose and freed his friend the antelope.

23 The Antelope Shows His Gratitude

The tortoise freed the antelope but his condition was critical. His mouth was bleeding and his teeth were almost falling off. So when the woodpecker hurried back to his friends to warn them about the hunter the antelope fled but the tortoise was too weak to move. When the hunter reached the spot he found the noose torn and seeing the tortoise lying there put him in a bag. Then throwing the bag on his shoulder he started off. The antelope observed everything from behind a thicket and quickly made a plan to rescue his friend. He came out of the bush and limped along until he caught the hunter's eyes. The hunter thought the antelope was injured and weak and ran after him leaving the bag under a tree. The antelope ran as fast as he could with the hunter chasing behind. When they had gone far he dodged the hunter and ran back to the lake by another path. He then tore open the bag freeing the tortoise. Before the hunter reached the spot the three friends ran back home.

24 The Robber and the Courtesan

The Bodhisattva was once a robber living in a village near Kasi. His activities brought him to the notice of the king and he was soon arrested. After the trial the king ordered the governor to put him to death. While the robber was being led to the execution site, Sama, the chief courtesan of the city, saw him and immediately fell in love. She sent word to the governor that the prisoner was her brother and bribed him with a thousand gold coins to set him free for a while. The governor, having accepted the bribe, complied with her wishes. Sama then persuaded an innocent youth who was madly in love with her to take the robber's place on the execution ground. So in place of the robber, the youth was executed. The robber was happy to be free but he couldn't trust Sama. "If she can kill her innocent admirer for me then she might kill me for someone else once she gets tired of me," thought he. So he went away from Kasi leaving Sama in despair.

25 The Story of Sabbadatha, the Jackal

Once upon a time, the Bodhisattva was the royal chaplain of Benaras. He was a highly knowledgeable man and knew a spell named Pathavijaya, which had the power to subdue the world. One day, while he was meditating in a lonely place he recited the spell and a jackal, hiding behind a thicket, overheard and learned it by heart. When the Bodhisattva finished his recital, the jackal appeared before him and said, "Ha! Ha! O Brahmin, I have learnt your spell. Now with its help, I'll take everyone under my control." The Bodhisattva tried to catch him but he escaped. With the help of the spell the jackal subdued all the creatures in the forest and became their king under the name Sabbadatha. Then he planned to capture the city of Benaras. "I'll take hold of the city by making my lions, who are already under my spell, roar," said Sabbadatha, sitting astride a lion which in turn stood on the back of two elephants.

26 The Bodhisattva Teaches Sabbadatha a Lesson

The Bodhisattva heard about the jackal's plans and asked everyone in the city to stuff their ears with flour so that the lions' roars wouldn't reach their ears. Then climbing the watchtower, he called out to the jackal, "Sabbadatha, stop trying to scare us. We want to see what you can do with your lions." These words enraged Sabbadatha and he ordered his lions to roar as loud as they could. So standing in front of the closed city gate, Sabbadatha's lions let out their earth-shaking roar. Even the lion, on which Sabbadatha sat, joined. His cry terrified the elephants and they dropped the lion from their back. Sabbadatha fell to the ground and got trampled under the elephants' feet. The Bodhisattva then said to the relieved king, "O king, knowledge is power but he who uses this power for a wrong purpose brings about his own ruin."

27 Sudata, Subahu and the Jackal

Once there lived in a forest a lion named Sudatha and a tiger named Subahu, who were close friends. One day a jackal, who used to live on the leftovers of these beasts, said to himself, "These two friends always share their food. If I can break their friendship, they won't share it anymore and I can get more leftovers from each. Moreover, they might take me for a well-wisher and give me more." Thinking this, the jackal went to each of the two and said that the other spoke evil about him. But both Sudatha and Subahu were too clever to believe the jackal blindly. They spoke with each other to know the truth and discovered that the jackal was lying. Having failed in his ploy, the jackal ran away.

28 King Bharu

Once there lived two groups of ascetics. One under a banyan tree towards the north of the city of Bharu and the other towards the south. The following year, the tree in the south withered away and the ascetics became homeless. Wandering the city for a new home, they reached the tree in the north and tried to drive away the ascetics who were already staying there. This led to a quarrel between the two groups whereupon the king was asked to solve the matter. The ascetics from the south bribed him and turned the judgment in their favour. Enraged at this injustice, the gods submerged the whole city under the sea leaving only the good people alive.

29 The Story of a Rooster

Once there lived a wise rooster in a forest where also lived a cunning cat who had killed many roosters but had never succeeded in harming the wise one. The cat planned a new way to catch him and one day, seeing the rooster on a high perch, stood below and started praising his good looks, pleading him to come down and take her as his wife. But the rooster was too wise to be deceived and replied, "Dear cat, you're wasting your time. I am not to be fooled by sweet words. I know your mean to kill me." Failing in her attempt, the cat went away.

30 A Hermit Called Kanha

Once there lived a pious brahmin called Kanha who gave away all his fortune to the poor and went to the Himalayas to live as an ascetic. There he practised strict meditation and acquired great spiritual powers. His power scared Sakka who feared that Kanha might take over his heavenly kingdom. One day, Sakka visited him and was impressed by Kanha's virtue and knowledge. "O pious soul, I offer your six boons of you choice. Tell me what you would like to have," said Sakka. But selfless as he was, Kanha only wished for his blessings so that he could stay virtuous forever and maintain his ascetic life. Pleased with him, Sakka decreed that the tree under which Kanha meditated should bear fruit forever.

Contents

The Story of the Month: Matribala's Power of Virtue

The Story of the Month

Matribala's Power of Virtue

01 Matribala's Power of Virtue

Once upon a time the Bodhisattva was born as a pious and kind-hearted king whose charity and humility were widely known. His prime concern was always the welfare of his subjects and he was ready to sacrifice anything for their protection. He was also very caring towards animals. He had a flawless sense of right and wrong and always gave judgments accordingly. He was thus respected by one and all and came to be known as Matribala, which meant "he whose strength is kindness". King Matribala's love for virtue had also influenced his subjects and they too followed the path of virtue. The kingdom of King Matribala was thus never disturbed by any criminal activities. The people were free from fear and enjoyed complete security.

One day, five *yakshas* whom Kubera, the king of *yakshas*, had banished from his kingdom due to some offence they had committed, reached the kingdom of King Matribala. These *yakshas* were wicked and never wished anyone any good. They felt jealous to see the people of the kingdom so happy and planned to bring misery upon them. They tried quite a few tricks to bring doom to the kingdom. But the power of virtue and the benevolence of the king acted as a magical shield for the people and the *yakshas* failed to harm them. They could not understand why they failed time and again. "It is strange that our power is useless here. But we must not give up. Rather let's find out what's actually stopping us from achieving our goal," they said to each other. So, taking the guise of poor Brahmins they started exploring the kingdom. After walking for long they reached a forest where they saw a lone shepherd boy resting under a large tree lost in thoughts. It seemed from his face that no fear, distrust or sorrow had ever touched him. The *yakshas* approached the boy and asked, "Dear boy, you are all alone in the forest. Aren't you scared?" "Scared?" questioned the shepherd boy, "Why do you think I should feel scared?" "Young man, haven't you heard about demons or *yakshas* who thrive on human flesh and blood? Even the bravest of the brave fear them. We wonder how you can find courage to sit here all alone," said the *yakshas*. Hearing this, the young man burst into laughter. "It seems you are new to this country. A magic shield protects our kingdom. It is not possible for even the gods to make a dent in this shield. So I find no reason to be afraid of any demons or *yakshas*," said he. "Pray, tell us what sort of magic shield is this that protects your kingdom from all danger," asked the *yakshas* eagerly. The shepherd smiled and told them about Matribala's power of virtue.

02 Yakshas Put Matribala to Test

The shepherd boy told the *yakshas* about Matribala. "Our magic shield is our king. His strength lies in his marvelous qualities like righteousness, kindness and selflessness. He has an army but he never uses force on anyone. In fact, such is his bearing that he enjoys the respect of all. He rules over his kingdom with such efficiency that even the wicked have given up the wrongful path. But why am I telling you all this? You should go to his capital and see for yourselves how happy the people are. They all follow the path of truth and virtue and never ever go astray. You will also see how kind they are to strangers," said he. Already annoyed with successive failures in corrupting the minds of the people, the *yakshas* got all the more infuriated at all this praise. They became determined to harm the king and came to his capital. They met the king in his court and said, "O great king, we have heard so much about your charity. Please give us some food."

03 Matribala's Dilemma

The king was delighted to get an opportunity to serve poor Brahmins. He immediately ordered his attendants to bring sumptuous dishes for them. Soon the *yakshas* were offered such good food that they had never seen in their lives. But wicked as they were they spurned the food and mockingly said, "Huh! What kind of food is this? O generous king, tell us whether you can serve us warm human flesh and warm blood for that is the food we are looking for." Saying this, they assumed their true selves. The whole court was startled to see the fearsome *yakshas*. The king realised that they were no human beings and they really meant what they had said. He was at a loss for what to do. At first he thought of killing the evil spirits but then he changed his mind considering the fact that they had come to his court asking for food no matter what they had at the back of their minds.

04 Matribala Agrees to Sacrifice Himself

The king's heart was filled with pity for these evil beings who, by treading the wrong path, were actually adding to their woes. He tried to think of a way to serve his guests with the kind of food they wanted. "Where shall I get fresh human flesh or blood?" wondered the king, "Neither can I refuse them food nor can I subject anyone to any kind of pain."
Suddenly he had an idea. He turned to the *yakshas* and said, "Friends, don't worry. I offer you my flesh and blood if they suit your purpose." Saying this, he ordered his physicians to cut flesh from his limbs and to open his veins so that warm blood could be served. The whole court and even the *yakshas* were amazed at his words. However, the viciousness of their minds stopped the *yakshas* from deterring the king. But the courtiers, to whom King Matribala was like a father, could not let this happen. They entreated the king not to grant the wish of the malicious *yakshas* saying that their actual intention was to harm the king and his kingdom.

05 Matribala Teaches Virtuosity

Hearing the objections of his subjects the king said, "My dear men, I know you are trying to stop me because you love me. But request me no more for I am determined to serve my guests. I have always taught you how to stick to the path of virtue. Then how can I act selfish and refuse to keep my promise?" Saying this, he gave the *yakshas* a big lump of his flesh and also his warm blood. Though in great pain, the king continued to wear a smile on his lips. The *yakshas* were too stunned to say anything. Then one of them asked the king, "O generous king, what do you get by adhering to your path of virtue?" "My dear, through these virtues I hope to get that knowledge with which I can free evil spirits from their harmful passions," replied the king. Hearing these words, the *yakshas* realised their mistake and asked for his forgiveness. Then they gave the king some magical herbs, which healed his wounds completely.

06 The Good Monkey and the Wicked Monkey

Once upon a time there lived a small red-faced monkey and a large black-faced monkey in a forest on the foothills of the mighty Himalayas. The smaller monkey was good-hearted and helpful. His goodness at times went to the extent of foolishness. On one occasion, it was raining heavily and the good-natured monkey sat safe inside his rock cave.

But the other monkey who lived on trees with his family was in trouble. Seeing the smaller monkey safe in his shelter, he made a plan. "Brother, will you be so kind as to give me shelter in your home?" he asked the smaller monkey. The latter was happy to help him. He welcomed the large monkey warmly but felt embarrassed, as he could not serve him any food. So he said, "O my friend, I am very sorry that I don't have any food to offer you. Please forgive me." The other monkey smiled and asked him not to feel embarrassed.

07 The Wicked Monkey Tricks the Good Monkey

The wicked monkey said to his embarrassed host, "Never mind my friend. Don't bother about food. I am very hungry no doubt, but what can you possibly do? Due to the heavy rain and storm there are no fruits left in the forest. I know about another forest where I am sure we would get plenty of food had it been possible for us to go there. But today in this heavy rain…" "Wait, my friend," the small monkey interrupted. "Are you sure that the place will have plenty of food? Then please tell me the way. I'll go and fetch food for both of us." Thus he went across to the other forest and gathering enough food, came back home. But alas! When he returned he found that the other monkey had brought in his family and together they had occupied the entire cave. The little monkey was thus thrown out of his own home because of his excessive goodness.

08 The Tricky Wolf and the Rats

Once upon a time there was a big rat who lived in a forest as the chief of thousands of other rats. In the same forest there lived a cunning wolf who had an *eye* on these rats. "It seems I won't have to bother about food for many days. Only thing I have to do is work out a perfect plan to catch them," thought the wolf as his mouth watered watching them. After thinking for a while, he came upon an idea. He went near the hole of the rats and waited until he saw them coming out. Then he stood with one front leg raised and mouth open. While crossing him the chief rat asked, "Why are you standing like this, dear wolf?" "O Rat, I am going through a bad phase. I have hurt my leg and can't put it down. So I have kept my mouth open to swallow air as I can't look for any food," replied the wolf with a sorry face.

09 The Rats Outwit the Tricky Wolf

The chief rat felt sorry for the poor wolf and started visiting him every day so that he felt good talking to them. But each time when they left, the wolf would eat up the last rat and stand there as before as if nothing had happened. After a few days, everyone started noticing that day by day the number of rats was dwindling and they guessed that the wolf was

responsible for it. So the chief called everyone and said, "Listen, my friends, we'll visit the wolf tomorrow just as usual. But this time I'll be the last one to leave." So the next day the rats visited him and when it was time for them to leave, the chief rat fell behind just as planned. The unsuspecting wolf pounced on him, but the rat was alert and slipped from under his paw. "You have failed this time, dear wolf. You can play no more tricks." Saying this, the rat sprang on the wolf's throat and bit him to death.

10 The Wise Monkey

Once upon a time there lived a wise monkey with a large band of followers. One summer day, while wandering in a forest, the monkeys felt thirsty and looked for water to drink. They found a large lake surrounded by a thicket of bamboos and were happily about to jump in when the wise monkey said, "Wait, my friends. Before we dive in, we should inspect the surroundings carefully. This place is new to us and there might be some danger lurking around." Saying this, the monkey went round the lake and examined the footprints on the bank. He noted with alarm that there were only footprints going down but none coming out of the water. "There must be a demon in this lake. It would not be safe to go into it. But don't worry. We'll manage to drink the water, anyway. Let's use these bamboos as straws and suck the water from above," suggested the monkey. So everyone picked up a bamboo and used it to drink to their fill.

11 The Merchant and the Vultures

Once, the Bodhisattva was born as a vulture named Gijjakutapabbata. One day, there was very heavy rainfall and Gijjakutapabbata and his friends had to take shelter in a ditch. As night fell, the vultures shivered out of hunger and cold. A merchant passing by saw the vultures and feeling pity, gave them fire and food to make themselves comfortable. When the storm was over, the vultures went back to their haunts but they did not forget the merchant's kindness. They decided to show him their gratitude. So they started picking up jewelleries and other precious things and dropping them in the merchant's garden. When the king came to know about this, he got Gijjakutapabbata caught. The merchant too was summoned and when the king came to know the truth, he released Gijjakutapabbata and asked the merchant to return the fineries back to the owners.

12 The Story of the Chaplain's Son

Once upon a time when King Susima ruled over Benaras, the Bodhisattva was the son of the royal chaplain who was also the master of the ceremonies of the elephant festival that used to take place in Benaras every year. After the chaplain's death, the priests, who all along coveted the honour of managing the prestigeous ceremonies, persuaded the king to give them the charge of the festival saying that his son was too young to shoulder the responsibility. One day, when only four days remained for the festival, the Bodhisattva found his mother crying and asked her why. She said, "My son, for so many years your father had the honour of being in charge of the elephant festival. This year your father is no more and it pains me to see that someone else is enjoying the honourable charge which is rightfully yours."

13 The Chaplain's Son Gains His Position of Honour

The Bodhisattva felt sorry for his mother and resolved to acquire all the knowledge that was needed to manage the elephant festival. He came to know about a renowned teacher in Takkasila who was an expert in elephants. He took his mother's blessings and went to the teacher and explained to him his purpose. Seeing the youth's urgency to uphold his family honour and fulfill his mother's dreams, the teacher promised to teach him everything he knew. As the Bodhisattva was extraordinarily intelligent and sincere, he learned all the elephant lore and the three Vedas in one night. The next morning he left for Benaras and reached there on the opening day of the festival. He met the king and protested against the violation of his rights. He challenged everyone present there to beat him in the knowledge of elephant lore and none could meet his challenge. Amazed at his immense knowledge, King Susima gave the Bodhisattva the right to supervise the ceremonies.

219

14 Asadisa, the skilled archer

The Bodhisattva was once born as Asadisa, the elder son of the king of Benaras. From a very tender age, he was keen on archery and became a skilled archer when he was a young boy. When his father died, Asadisa made his younger brother the king as he was disinterested in royal power. After a while, Asadisa realised that his brother feared that he might ask back the throne and thus left his kingdom to put an end to his brother's anxiety. He became an archer in the army of a neighbouring king. Soon he rose to the rank of the chief archer due to his extraordinary skills. On one occasion, he brought down a mango from a tree with the downward motion of his arrow which when shooting up had crossed the first level of Heaven. He attained great fame and his name spread far and wide.

15 The Brave Asidasa

The kings of seven neighbouring states together once attacked the kingdom of Benaras. The news of this sudden attack reached Asidasa and he resolved to help his country in its hour of crisis. Taking his leave from the king, Asidasa reached Benaras and went straight to the tent where the seven kings were having their dinner, defeating every opposition that came in his way. He broke all the seven plates in which the kings were having their food with only one miraculous shot from his arrow. Terrified, the kings immediately retreated. When the news reached Benaras, the king immediately rushed to the scene and welcomed Asidasa warmly. In gratitude, he asked Asidasa to take up the throne. But Asidasa declined the offer and then, renouncing worldly life, became an ascetic.

16 The Elephant with Six Tusks

Once upon a time the Bodhisattva was born as Uposatha, the king of the Chaddanta elephants who were considered to have the highest rank among elephants. The majestic elephant was known for his handsome white body, red face and feet and six shining tusks. He lived deep inside a forest along with his two wives Mahasubhadda and Chullasubhadda. One day, after bathing in the river that flowed through the forest, Uposatha was frolicking with his wives in the forest and playfully hit a big sal tree with his trunk. The blow shook the tree and beautiful flowers rained on Mahasubhadda whereas dry twigs, leaves and red ants fell on Chullasubhadda. Chullasubhadda felt very insulted and rejecting all the pleas of her husband, she left him. In due course Chullasubhadda died and was reborn as a princess in the royal family of Madda. When she came of age, she became the chief queen of Varanasi and planned to avenge her insult.

17 Chullasubhadda Plans to Harm the Elephant with Six Tusks

Chullasubhadda was reborn as a princess but still remembered her past life. She still fumed when she thought of the humiliation her previous husband had caused her. She secretly planned to have the six tusks of the elephant cut off. After much pleading, she convinced her husband to get the tusks for her with which she said she would make some fine ornaments. The king thus summoned Sonuttara, the chief hunter of his kingdom, to find the elephant and cut his six tusks off. It took seven long years for Sonuttara to locate the home of the elephant king. He then dug a big pit near his abode and covered it with dry leaves and twigs. The unsuspecting Chaddanta king stepped on the trap and fell into the pit. As soon as he was caught, the hunter aimed a poisonous arrow at him. But such was the vigour of the elephant that even in this dire condition, he got up and charged at the hunter.

18 Chullasubhadda Died in Penance

King Elephant fought hard with the hunter. However, when he noticed that the hunter was dressed in saffron robes like a monk, he stepped back and stopped his fight out of respect for the holy colour. Sonuttara was moved to tears by his deep piety and brushing aside his assignment, divulged everything to the elephant. Hearing him, King Elephant volunteered to cut off his beautiful tusks so as to save Sonuttara from the severe punishment that he would face if he failed to bring the six tusks for the queen. He thus sawed off his own tusks and handed them over to the hunter. With a heavy heart, the hunter went back to Varanasi and presented them to the queen. By then, Chullasubhadda, was already regretting her decision and her heart was filled with deep remorse. When the hunter showed her the tusks, she could not bear the horror of the sight and died in grief.

19 False Admiration

Once, the Bodhisattva was born as a tree sprite living in a jambu tree in the middle of a deep forest. On the same tree a crow lived happily feeding on its juicy fruits. One day, a jackal happened to come by looking for food. His eyes fell on the jambu tree and his mouth watered seeing the succulent fruits. "Oh! These must be delicious. I'll climb the tree and get those fruits. There can't be any better food than these fruits," thought the jackal. But every time he tried to climb the tree, he slipped down. Failing in his first efforts, the jackal thought of another way to get the fruits. He saw the crow on the tree and suddenly got an idea. "Hello, Mr Crow! How do you do? Have you observed today's weather? It's so nice. It would be all the better if I have the privilege to listen to your joyful song," said the jackal trying to flatter the crow.

20 The Tree Sprite Drives Away the False Admirers

The crow was delighted with the jackal's compliment as no one had ever praised him so. But holding back his joy, he asked the jackal, "Well, Mr. Jackal. It's nice to hear your compliment. But are you sure you want to listen to my song?" "Of course, I am sure. Good food and good music—what more do you want in life?" said the jackal. Pleased with his words, the crow said, "O Mr Jackal, you seem to be very wise. First, taste these delicious fruits and then I'll sing to you." Saying this, he began to drop the fruits from the tree for the jackal to eat. "Mr Jackal, you are the most endearing person I have ever met. I really don't understand why all the animals have selected Mr Lion as your king instead of you," said the crow expecting more compliments from the jackal as the latter went on eating the fruits greedily. This false mutual flattery continued till it became unbearable for the tree sprite and he drove away the two liars.

21 The Virtuous Man

Once, the Bodhisattva was born as a famous teacher who was respected for his wisdom and knowlege. One day, a man came to him with a unique problem. He had four beautiful and virtuous daughters of marriageable age but did not know whether to look for beauty, nature, nobility or virtue in the prospective grooms. So he asked the Bodhisattva for advice. Learning about all the qualities of the suitors, the Bodhisattva said, "Handsome features will wither with time, experience—anyone can gather gradually, noble lineage does not ensure that the man will be noble. But virtuousness is the only quality that really matters. A man's virtues remains even after his death as a person is always remembered for his good deeds." Hearing this, the Brahmin married off all of his four daughters to a virtuous man.

22 The old woman and her son

Once, there lived a mother and a son who were very devoted to each other. Their mutual love made the son's wife very jealous. She felt that her husband loved his mother more than he loved her. After much scheming she at last became successful in throwing her mother-in-law out of the house. Later a child was born to the young couple and the woman went around telling everyone that had her mother-in-law been present in the house, she would never have been blessed with such a beautiful child. When these words reached the old woman she became very upset. "My daughter-in-law behaves so shamelessly because Justice is dead," thought she and went to the cemetery to perform a sacrifice in the memory of Justice. As soon as she started the sacrifice, the heavenly throne of Sakka started shaking. He came down to Earth to see what the matter was. After hearing the old woman's sorrowful tale, he chastised her daughter-in-law. The latter then realised her mistake and reunited the old woman with her son.

23 The Wise Goat and the Wolf

Once upon a time a herd of wild goats lived in a cave by the hillside. Not far from it there lived a family of wolves. The wolf and his mate always had their eyes on these goats and one by had eaten them all up except one. Being very wise the lone goat had successfully evaded every danger. One day, the he-wolf said to his wife, "My dear, we have only this clever goat left to eat. I have a plan. If we can carry it out successfully, the goat will not be able to escape." According to his plan, the male wolf lay down on the ground pretending to be dead. His mate went to the cave and called the goat. "Dear Goat, please help me! My husband has died leaving me all alone. I know we have killed your friends. But the situation has changed now. Will you be so kind as to come with me and help me bury my dear husband?" cried the she-wolf all in tears.

24 The Wise Goat Saves Herself

The goat felt sorry for the wolf crying for help. But wise as she was she was wary too. "This might be a trap. Should I trust her?" wondered she. Then, answering the wolf from inside the cave, she said, "Dear Wolf, I feel sorry for you. But I don't think I should trust you. So please go and ask your friends for help." "O good Goat, please don't refuse me. I am all alone here with no family or friends," said the wolf weeping miserably. Her pitiable words aroused sympathy in the goat's heart and she finally agreed. Still she tried to be careful and said, "I'll come with you, dear Wolf. But I want you to lead the way." And thus they went up the hillside to the spot where the he-wolf was lying. As soon he heard footsteps, he raised his head so as to see them. The goat, who was keeping a comfortable distance between herself and the she-wolf, saw the he-wolf raise his head. Realising that her suspicion was true, she immediately turned back and ran away.

25 The Wise Goat Scares Away the Wolf

The she-wolf was angry with her husband for having failed to catch the wise goat and reproached him for raising his head and missing the golden chance of catching the goat. But her husband still didn't lose hope and made a new plan. Next day, the she-wolf went up to the goat and said, "O good goat, I am so thankful to you. I thought my husband was dead. But your auspicious presence brought him back from a near-death condition. Come with me to our home and let's be friends." But this time the goat didn't believe her and decided to play a trick to drive the cunning wolves off. So with a smile the goat said, "O dear wolf, you don't have to thank me. I accept your invitation. You go back first. I'll follow with my friends—two hounds, and that big dog named Four Eyes." Hearing about her friends, the wolf got very scared and ran away.

26 Auspicious Words

Once, the Bodhisattva was born as a rich and famous merchant. One day, while he was away in a distant land on business, his mother-in-law visited his home. Now, the old woman was nearly deaf and could faintly hear a few words. After the initial greeting, the woman asked her daughter if she was happy with her husband. "O mother, I am too well. My husband is possibly the best person one has ever met. He is calm and noble like a hermit," replied the daughter delightfully. However, her mother could not hear anything. Her ears could only catch the word 'hermit' faintly. Thinking that her son-in-law had turned a sage leaving her daughter in misery, the woman started wailing, "Oh destiny, how cruel had you been with my darling daughter. Now she has to lead a life of a hermit's wife in the forest…" Her pitiable cries caught the ears of the neighbours and before long, the news spread as a wildfire that the merchant had turned a sage. Meanwhile, the merchant was on his way home with loads of gifts for his wife. On the way, he met one of his neighbours who bowed before him and said, "O noble soul, you are indeed great to have left all the luxuries of life and become a sage at this young words." Hearing this, the merchant felt that these auspicious words of his turning an ascetic should not be proved wrong and so he actually became a sage.

27 The Fox and the Piece of Meat

Once upon a time a hungry fox who had not eaten for several days found a piece of flesh. He eagerly took it in his mouth and started off for his den. On his way he happened to pass by a hen yard. His eyes fell on two fat fowls and his mouth watered to see them. He put the piece of meat on the ground and sat down staring at them longingly. He was in utter confusion as to whether he should resmain content with the piece of meat or go for the fowls. Just then a jackal was passing by and stopped to see the fox sitting there with a perplexed face. "What's the matter with you, Dear Fox? Can I help you in any way?" asked the jackal. The fox told him about his confusion.

28 The Fox Pays for His Greediness

The Jackal listened as the fox told him about his confusion and said, "Too much greed is bad, Dear Fox. Moreover, a boy watches over these fowls. So be content with what you have as one in hand is always better than two in the bush." But still the fox was in two minds and, finally, ignoring the advice of the jackal, went to catch the fowls leaving the piece of meat on the ground. Just as he neared one fowl, a boy suddenly appeared and hit him with a big stick. The fox ran away and saved his life. But when he rushed back to the spot where he had left his meat, he was shocked to see no trace of it anywhere as a few moments ago a kite, who was flying over the place, had carried the meat to her nest.

29   The Poor Village Doctor

One warm afternoon, some village boys were playing near a tree when a poor village doctor was on his way back home after a visit to his patient's house. He was very upset as the patient, being very poor, couldn't give him his fees. When he saw the boys playing, an idea suddenly crossed his mind. The doctor knew that in a hollow of that tree lived a poisonous snake. To make some money he told the boys, "Do you want to catch a hedgehog? There is one in that hollow." One boy, who was actually the Bodhisattva, innocently put his hand into the hollow. But as soon as he did so, he felt the snake. Showing great presence of mind, the boy grabbed the snake by its neck and flung it away from him. The snake fell on the doctor and bit him to death.

30   The Sound the Hare Heard

One day, a foolish hare was sitting under a belli tree when a belli fruit fell on the ground with a loud "thud!" The sound startled the hare and he started running away thinking the earth was breaking up. Seeing him run for life another hare shouted, "What's the matter with you?" "The earth is breaking up," yelled back the hare as he kept on running. The other hare got scared and he too started running. Soon the panic spread over the entire jungle and all the animals started running without knowing where they headed. Only King Lion kept his cool. He stopped the scared animals and said, "My dear subjects, the earth is not breaking. Come with me and let's check the place again." They all went back to the place and found a big belli fruit on the ground. All the animals then realised that they had foolishly given too much importance to rumours.

31 The Beautiful Asanka

Once an ascetic found a beautiful baby girl amongst a bunch of lotuses in a pond and reared her up as his daughter. He named her as Asanka, under the name of a creeper for whose fruits gods waited for a thousand years. Asanka grew up to be a beautiful maiden and everyone loved her for her kind and loving nature. One day, King Brahmadatta of Benaras came to hunt in the same forest where Asanka lived with her father. Asanka was plucking some wild flowers a little distance away from her hut when king Brahmadatta saw her and immediately fell in love with her. "I must have this beautiful lady as my wife," thought the king and followed her to her hut. The ascetic was surprised to see the king at his doorstep and when the king revealed his desire to marry Asanka, the ascetic laid a condition that he would only give his daughter's hand in marriage with the king if the latter could guess her name. Knowing this, Asanka who had also liked the king coyly gave the hint that her name was after a creeper which was abundant in the forest. But the king failed to guess it. Then the girl mentioning her name in her conversation told the king that the word had occurred during the talk. The king thought hard until he remembered it. He then met the ascetic and told the name and before long, the king was married to Asanka.